NORA GALLAGHER

PRACTICING RESURRECTION

Nora Gallagher's bestselling memoir, *Things Seen and Unseen: A Year Lived in Faith,* received outstanding reviews. Her essays, book reviews, and journalism have appeared in many publications, including *The New York Times Magazine, The Washington Post, Double-Take, Time,* the *Los Angeles Times Magazine, The Village Voice,* and *Mother Jones.* She is also the editor of the award-winning *Patagonia: Notes from the Field,* a collection of literary essays on the outdoors. She and her husband live in Santa Barbara, California.

ALSO BY NORA GALLAGHER

Things Seen and Unseen: A Year Lived in Faith

PRACTICING
RESURRECTION

PRACTICING RESURRECTION

A Memoir of Work, Doubt, Discernment,

and Moments of Grace

NORA GALLAGHER

Vintage Books · A Division of Random House, Inc. · New York

FIRST VINTAGE BOOKS EDITION, JANUARY 2004

Grateful acknowledgment is made to the following for
permission to reprint previously published material:
North Point Press and Wendell Berry: Excerpt from the poem "Manifesto:
The Mad Farmer Liberation Front" from *Collected Poems: 1957–1982* by
Wendell Berry. Copyright © 1985 by Wendell Berry. Reprinted by
permission of North Point Press, a division of Farrar, Straus and Giroux,
LLC and the author.
Random House Children's Books: Excerpt from *Oh Say Can You Say?* by
Dr. Seuss. TM and Copyright © by Dr. Seuss Enterprises, L.P. 1979.
Reprinted by permission of Random House Children's Books,
a division of Random House, Inc.

The Library of Congress has cataloged the Knopf edition as follows:
Gallagher, Nora.
Practicing resurrection : a memoir of work, doubt, discernment,
and moments of grace / Nora Gallagher.—1st ed.
p.   cm.
ISBN 0-375-40594-1
2002114928

Vintage ISBN: 0-375-70563-5

Book design by Dorothy S. Baker

www.vintagebooks.com

Printed in the United States of America
10   9   8   7   6   5   4   3   2   1

For Vincent, Anne, and Harriet

... Be like the fox
who makes more tracks than necessary,
some in the wrong direction.
Practice resurrection.

—*Manifesto: The Mad Farmer Liberation Front,*
   by Wendell Berry

Some of the names in this book have been changed.

CONTENTS

The prayer books illuminated for gentry in the Middle Ages were called Books of Hours. Hours or "offices" were set aside throughout the day, during which prayers were said to commemorate the Virgin, the Passion, the Cross, the Holy Spirit, and the dead. In them drawings invade the pages, sometimes the very words of prayers. In a Book of Hours made for a young French queen, a cluster of angels crowds into an attic, lines of daily offices morph into a gazelle, a juggler balancing a plate, a beggar holding his bowl. In the prayer said for St. Louis, a rabbit hides within the letter B, eating a cabbage leaf. Words become flesh. It's as if the scribes who made these books could not resist pairing the world—its loveliness, its mystery, its dailiness—with the *Adoramus te* of prayer and supplication.

PRACTICING

RESURRECTION

OVERTURE

In mid-November of 1995, during the church season of ordinary time, my brother's radiologist told him he had "zero percent" chance of recovery from the cancer diagnosed only a year earlier. Our family went into a kind of free-fall, and my religious faith took a series of unexpected turns. The year itself was filled with change: Kit underwent all the horrors of surgery, chemotherapy, and pain; the newly hired priest at my church began the hard work of reviving a parish; I worked with homeless men and women in the church soup kitchen.

I had been part of the community at Trinity Episcopal Church for six years and I had finally begun to see that my faith was not about belief in something irrational or about a blind connection to something unreal or about "belief" at all. As I worked in the soup kitchen, tried to pray, planned liturgies, and dealt with my brother's illness, what I came to understand was that my faith had to be grounded in experience, or in "impulses," as Simone Weil put it, "of an essentially and manifestly different order." Faith for me was about the accumulation of these experiences, not abstractions, not believing, as the White Queen said to Alice, "six impossible things before breakfast."

The life of faith was amorphous, ephemeral, a glimpse, a moment. Trusting it was like my early swimming lessons in learning how to float.

The agony my brother and our family were undergoing was also like a kind of fire, the purification talked of by mystics and saints. I felt as if old layers of myself were being seared to ash, and my skin was raw and baby soft. I began to explore my role in the church and in the world, the "reason I was put here on this planet," as a friend said, asking myself what I was "called" to do as the world I had understood and grown up in was being shattered and burned.

Beginning in the early fall, I met with four laypeople for three hours once a month. They were called a discernment committee; the Episcopal Diocese of Los Angeles (and many other dioceses) requires that a person who senses a "call" to ordained ministry examine that call with a group of peers within his or her parish for one year.

Discernment is a hard subject to define or pin down. Lee McGee, a priest who is a retired professor of pastoral theology at Yale Divinity School and did ground-breaking work on women and preaching, said discernment is partly about "lowering the volume on some voices; upping it on others." We consulted a book called *Listening Hearts,* which had pointers on discernment, and I asked a Quaker friend how they discerned. She replied, "Well, basically we sit in silence." An Episcopal priest who visited Trinity gave us a tip in his sermon: "Often we are afraid to ask for what we want or desire," said Carr Holland, "but the way of discernment is to lay out our desire and then come back to it with openness, seeking the wisdom of examination. Is this a need? Is there a deeper need? Is your reign foreshadowed here?"

If someone from outside the church had been a fly on the wall during our discernment sessions, she or he would have seen five people sitting together around various dining-room tables mostly in silence. Every now and then, someone would speak. If anything was an example of how the church differs from the secular, this was it. We sat. We waited. I am not sure any of us knew what exactly we were doing in the beginning—we had no "training"—but we took to it, awkwardly at first and then more easily, as if returning to an old, ill-used language.

.   `   .

As the year wore on, we became more familiar with what I came to call "the pull." A particular image or question would rise in the mind and would not fade: it felt the way a fishing line feels when a trout takes the hook below the surface, that singular tug, differing so much from a snag on a weed, of a living, breathing creature.

The bottom line was that we had to sit in silence for hours. We had to train our ears to hear what wasn't there. Mark Benson said that one session that fall reminded him of the movie *Poltergeist:* "a room with things flying around in it in slow motion." We had to bet on the irrational or at least on what could not be explained by the rational, could not be seen or nailed down. For this reason, we had to be very careful of sloppiness, sentimentality, or jumping to conclusions out of impatience or fear. After a while, I began to think of it as refining hunch.

All of this seeking out and holding a sense of a greater reality, and its meaning and my suffering over my brother took place in, and could not have taken place without, my "community of faith," Trinity Church in Santa Barbara, a place that was growing and changing under the leadership of the priest, Mark Asman, and the laypeople of the church. We too were being purified by fire: the leadership of the church had been told that Mark was gay; the larger congregation had not. The suffering in Mark's past, his decision to come out to himself and to the leaders of the church, forced all of us to reconsider the role of the church in the world, and in our own lives. We could not be a nice social club or, as Philip Turner, former dean at Yale Divinity School, put it, "a lonely crowd in pursuit of private ends." We had to understand the old roles of the church: as witness, as prophet, as place of fire.

In early December that year, early Advent by the church calendar, I took the labyrinth, a 30' × 30' piece of cotton canvas on which was painted an elaborate circular path, a medieval walking meditation, down to the Diocesan Convention in Riverside, California. We laid it down in an upstairs room, which overlooked the floor of the convention. Below us, elected lay delegates, along with priests and bishops, clashed and argued, voted on resolutions, and generally demonstrated the politics of the church. I saw both sides of the vocation that day. On the labyrinth, priests, men, and women wearing largely black, with that slash of white at the throat, walked in deep thought in deep prayer in silence, hands held behind the back. How serious they looked to me, how full of longing. And then, as I glanced through a window to the floor below, I saw the other side acted out, sometimes by the same people I had earlier watched on the labyrinth: nervous men and women shuffling papers, waiting at the microphone, networking with each other and with the bishops in corners of the room.

A vocation. From the Latin *vocare,* to call. Here I was in the throes of deciding whether or not I was called, a term that made me cringe, to the priesthood, a profession, a loving friend had pointed out, that paid even less than that of writing. This call or whatever it was had disrupted my marriage, confused my friends, and forced to the surface most of my hidden neuroses. It had landed on me in the middle of my life, a suspicious mid-life crisis, and yet, and yet. In that room above the convention hall, more than a hundred people throughout the day walked in silence. As I watched them pass each other in their stocking feet, I thought of centuries of pilgrims walking toward shrines or other holy places, hoping and knowing that somehow in the journey itself, in the seeking, one would find the dwelling place, heaven's gate.

THE OFFICE

OF THE DEAD

❦

1996

1

I have a recurring dream in which I find, behind the familiar walls of my study or bedroom, another whole house. It is always much bigger and grander than the house I live in. Once its long windows looked out on fields of lavender in Provence. In the dream I think, Why didn't I figure this out before? It's simply a matter of finding a door.

I sat in church near the altar on a Thursday evening in April, waiting for it all to begin. Watery blue light fell from the high windows onto the fair linen, empty as a pocket. The altar was wooden and plain, ordered from a Lutheran catalog specializing in church furniture. The wine, shortly to sit on the altar in a little silver chalice that a priest found in a second-hand store, was cheap Christian Brothers cream sherry; the wafers were the whole wheat variety made by nuns in Clyde, Missouri. The table, the wine, the wafers were as everyday, as ordinary as my house, and also contained within and behind them a reality as complex, as beautiful, and as hidden as the house in my dream.

Prayers rose from the kneelers; I breathed in the stone-cooled air. In a few minutes, others arrived for this Thursday-evening service. An attorney for legal aid, an advocate for abused children, a heating serviceman, a realtor. Someone new, a woman with short reddish-brown hair wearing a cream-colored suit. They walked in from the street and stood in the cool dark, looking momentarily lost or disoriented, as if they had crossed a border and were in need of new currency, and then sat down.

Mark Asman, our parish priest, arrived last, in a black suit, clerical shirt, and collar. In Mark's breast pocket was a small leather church calendar in which he kept, in a round, scrawled hand, dates for meetings on the pages marked with the names of martyrs and saints. On that calendar was a meeting on "human sexuality," scheduled for June 11, a feast day for St. Barnabas, an apostle.

As Mark settled in, a stranger with dirty clothes and a stubbled chin walked unevenly into the church and sat down in a shadowed pew. He had "homeless" written all over him. Probably drunk. Mark motioned for him to come up to the altar area. He staggered slightly as he climbed the steps. When we stood for the Gospel reading, he reached for Mark's hand and held onto it, his fingers knotted with Mark's like lovers, for the rest of the service.

Ann Jaqua, a laywoman, gathered up her notes and headed for the lectern. The theme for her homily that night was "Mysticism 101."

"Here at the end of the twentieth century, we have difficulty with anything that is neither apparent to the senses nor obvious to the intelligence," Ann began. "We are caught in a restricted way of knowing that the scientific world has given us. And, as Huston Smith says, the scientific method only measures those aspects of reality we can control, leaving out all those aspects that are beyond our ability to control. All things that exceed us in freedom, intelligence, and purpose, things that cannot be pinned down."

After the sermon and the peace, Anne Howard, the priest who was celebrating that night, held her palms over the bread and wine. She said, "Breathe on these bodily things."

People asked for prayers: for my daughter who has eczema on her hands; in thanksgiving for my sister who, so far, is enduring chemo, her hair has not fallen out; I asked for prayers for the soul of my brother, Kit, and stood in their midst shaking with tears. They held their palms like light wings over my back and shoulders. Anne rubbed oil that smelled of rosemary into my forehead, and made the sign of the cross. Breathe on us.

When Anne raised her hand to bless us at the end of the service, the drunk raised his hand, too, and, right along with her, made the sign of the cross over us all. We were there, empty as the altar, becoming flesh.

When my husband, Vincent, and I came home from New Mexico after Kit's death, cards from the people at church were stacked up on the white table next to our front door like leaves on a lawn. Mark Benson, who served on my discernment committee, read a verse from Dr. Seuss into the answering machine and I scribbled it on a scrap of paper from my brother's house: " 'The storm starts when the drops start dropping. When the drops stop dropping, then the storm starts stopping.' It feels to me like what grief is like."

Outside, green lawns and ivy, fields of yellow mustard, wild lilac loosed on the hills, palm trees, and beach sand. It was not like New Mexico where Kit and I grew up and where I had just left his ashes. In New Mexico dark mesas rise off the desert floor, heart-shaped leaves of cottonwoods dance by the river, orchards are fed by each village's *acequia madre,* the mother ditch.

I dreamed of a piece of pottery I found on land I own near Santa Fe. It was colored gray, like ashes, and had the remains of a design on it, a black V. I thought of the people who had made that jar, walking, then falling, their bones intertwined in the roots of the sagebrush under my feet, and then I put it back where I had found it, in a streambed fed by summer rains.

A bouquet of flowers arrived from the monks at Mt. Calvary monastery. The card read, "With love from your brothers."

Vincent and I couldn't do simple things. We couldn't go to the grocery store or cook dinner. On our first night back, an insulated carry-all appeared on the front porch, left there by

Dodie Little, from Trinity. Inside was a cooked chicken, potato salad, green beans, and brownies. I realized that had she not brought it to us, we would not have eaten.

In the week ahead, I could hardly bear to be in church. I couldn't be in large rooms or with many people at once. I suffocated on the living. I believed no one noticed, until Mark Asman took me aside and said, "Are you having trouble with crowds since Kit died?"

I felt as if I was wandering around in a newly discovered archeological dig where there are pieces of things all over the ground—pottery shards, abandoned campsites, and bones—and that someday someone would come along and make sense of them.

I would be watering the garden or opening an envelope and Kit's death would spring on me completely new and jolting, as if I'd been hit hard from behind with no warning, and I then would fold up, like a fan.

Parts of my life, the life I led before Kit grew sick and died, no longer made sense. A life of meetings, stretched between appointments, always ten minutes late. Half listening to people. A life dictated by clocks and money and computers and cars, without hawks and lakes and wild roses, a world increasingly without surprise or humor. I thought of how we as a species have endangered not only animals and plants around us, but the wild nature of our own lives. We have fabricated this world, to paraphrase the writer Philip Sherrard, and our punishment is that we have to adapt to it.

I half realized, as I stood in the wreckage of my brother's death, that I had lost more than Kit; I'd lost my own wild life, I'd lost the sacred in the world. By the life I was leading, I had lost much of the holy, and my job now, if one could call it a job, was to find it again but in a different place.

I thought of a story about Dan Corrigan, a retired Episcopal bishop. Dan was famous in the church for breaking rules. He had been arrested during the Vietnam War for saying Mass on the Pentagon steps, had advocated the ordination of homosexuals in the fifties, and had been nearly shot by a Mississippi state trooper when he went down to speak of civil rights at a black college in 1952. He and other bishops and priests spoke for the ordination of women to the priesthood from the late sixties onward, but the national church's governing bodies did not act. In 1974, after much deliberation, conversation, and prayer, he and two other bishops stepped into the breach and ordained eleven women to the Episcopal priesthood in Philadelphia, without benefit of church permission, risking censure and revocation of their licenses to preach and preside. Dan was in his eighties at the time.

Anne Howard was saying goodbye to Dan one day up at the monastery.

"Take care of yourself, Dan," said Anne, turning to walk out the door.

Dan stopped, and said, "No, I don't think so."

"I beg your pardon?" Anne asked.

"I don't take care of myself," Dan replied. "I spend myself."

I felt an urgency to reclaim the holy in my life, to find a new way to spend myself. Kit's death gave that desire weight, a kind of gravity. His death and its aftermath were benchmarks against which I measured the clarity or falsehood of my next steps, the next path.

And thus I set out to do something new as a way to come to myself, a new way to spend myself.

Since Kit's death, I have been visited—there is no other word for it—by birds. Driving north on Highway 101, a red-tailed hawk flies low over the hood of my car, so close I can see the black bead of his eye. Sitting in a garden of a retreat house near Malibu, the wide Pacific Ocean spread before me, a hummingbird zips to within a foot of my face. The day of Kit's death, I found myself, without knowing how I got there, standing in the midst of a bird refuge near his house, listening to the ducks in the rushes and millet, and watching the movement of wind on the water. I could not make sense of these events, but they had the quality of something larger, or deeper, Simone Weil's "events of a different order." They, too, counted in my next decision, although I did not know how or why.

In the midst of this year of discernment, as I sat with those four people, four other souls, for three hours once a month and listened for the word of God that was often like the sound of wind, or the motion of birds, I knew that Kit's death echoed into this. His death had a wake, the way everything has a sound.

It started for me as a series of dreams. In each of them, I served the Eucharist bread, the bread or wafers that can be blessed only by a priest. (A priest consecrates the bread, but this consecration can't be done alone. The Eucharist must be celebrated in community.)

I was never inside a church, I was always walking outside, sometimes in the countryside, sometimes in city streets. Once, I served rice. A few grains in my palm became a never-ending supply, a fine puffy mound, as long as I gave it away. I served it to groups of people standing on the street. As I lifted my palm to a woman dressed in a neat black suit, diamond earrings, and a red fox coat and offered, politely, "The Body of Christ?" she said, "Oh, yes, I could use that."

In one dream, I sifted through a covered tray for bits of bread to serve. The tray was like one my mother used at cocktail parties to collect ashes and cigarette butts. I had to be careful to distinguish between the wafers and the trash. It was very important to get everyone fed, and on the right food. In another, I held Jesus' coat. In yet a third, Nelson Mandela, who was giving the homily at Trinity, for some dream-like reason, turned to me and said, "And when are we going to get you preaching?"

Whatever it was, it did not go away. Mark Benson sent me a card with a medieval woodcut of a shepherd carrying a particularly nasty-looking child on his shoulders up a steep canyon, with the inscription, "Get off my back, Jesus." Inside Mark wrote, "Is the Hound of Heaven hounding you?"

Any person serious about her faith has probably looked up from pew or chair and thought, I wonder what it's like to be . . . up there? To dedicate one's life to the celebration at the altar, to be at the heart of life-changing events of people's lives, to make a difference. To go all the way. Not to mention getting focused attention, wielding power, and wearing those great clothes. And also—I would learn much more about this over the next three years—after you've been a member of a faith community for some time, you begin to wonder, Isn't there something besides sitting down, standing up, and singing? Isn't there anything more?

I sought what Ann Jaqua calls my true self, or some kind of completion. I feared what Rilke called the "repository of unlived lives." I knew I wanted to do this with my community and in my community. I did not want to be the Lone Ranger.

After Mark Asman had been at Trinity only a month, I made an appointment to speak to him.

We sat down in his office. I had made the date without saying what it was about. He told me later he had thought I wanted to complain to him about something he'd done in his first few weeks in the parish.

"I like the way you've moved the furniture around in this office," I said, in my usual pitiful attempt at small talk.

"Thank you," he replied, shuffling papers on his desk. It didn't occur to me that Mark was afraid of me, and it didn't occur to Mark that I was afraid of him. Into this crowded atmosphere I whispered, "I think, I might be thinking about a possible, a possible . . ."

"Cut to the chase," he said.

"Priesthood," I said.

"Oh," he said, practically wiping his brow with relief. "Well, let's take a look at that." We talked about my dreams, my various roles in the church, the institutional demands of priesthood. I had been a part of the Episcopal church since I was a young teenager, baptized at the age of fifteen at St. John's Cathedral in Albuquerque, New Mexico. I had left the church, like so many of my generation, in my twenties, returning in the late 1970s, to a small church in San Francisco. Since then I had served on a bishop's committee in a mission church in Colorado, worked in the soup kitchen at Trinity, and was soon to be elected to the vestry (the name given to the board of a church) at Trinity. Finally Mark said carefully, "I don't think it's off the map. It's not usually something that is immediately known, as if you would have a vision or something and that would be the end of it. We are all becoming what we are called to be."

As I got up to leave, he said, "One thing: a priest must love herself."

"I'm not sure I do," I replied.

"I'm not sure I do, either," he said and smiled.

Mark and I sat down together in the next weeks and chose the discernment committee. I chose them as if picking a team for the spiritual Olympics: Mark Benson was a physician assistant, the first openly gay member of the vestry at All Saints, Pasadena, the largest Episcopal church on the West Coast, and the first man to have his partnership blessed in a public ceremony at that church in 1992 (Phil died later that year); Elizabeth Corrigan, ninety-three, widow of Dan Corrigan, who counted among her friends and acquaintances Dorothy Day and Daniel Berrigan; Ed Potts, a college administrator with a soft and permeable heart; and Ann Jaqua, who had logged fifty years in the church and been a spiritual director for ten years, and was the kind of woman who analyzed visions and dreams as if they were stock tables. Each of the four embodied qualities of discernment.

Ann has gray curly hair and beautiful papery skin. She bought her clothes at secondhand stores, picking up linen shirts and dresses for a quarter of their original price. She once made a birthday table setting for me out of lambs' ears and white roses. In England, she bought paint of a particular hue of blue, a kind of robin's egg blue, and painted the inside shelves of a second-hand cabinet with glass doors in which she keeps linens.

Once she came over to see me and began automatically weeding my rose garden. Ann's husband, David Griffin, is a theologian; their West Highland terrier, Evey, is named after Alfred North Whitehead's wife, Evelyn.

Ann's years of listening to people in spiritual direction had taught her to avoid supernatural language and imagery. She resisted, as I did, the word "call."

"If you use supernatural language, then you end up waiting for that one big lightning bolt, instead of sticking to your own life, to what your own life is about, step by step," she said. " 'Call' makes you think of a voice from outer space, which it is not. These voices are in us already. They are drowned out or muffled. Discernment is about cleaning up the clutter to find the thread."

Mark Benson had the patience of a gardener. I had watched him prepare his south-facing slope for a rose garden: hours digging trenches, the purchase of manure and peat moss, the selection of David Austin bare roots, and I had seen the result—roses the size of dinner plates. His patience was no mealy-mouthed "Christian" ethic. It had the cut of steel. When he was ready, he acted. I don't think a locomotive could have stopped his decision to marry Philip in public.

Elizabeth had a rare wisdom that was bodily experience. She

had taken her whole life into her body, and let it reflect there, among her cells, checking it for truth or falsity. Her husband had been a priest, and then a bishop, and she knew the costs of his vocation.

Ed Potts knew exactly when to move and when to stay put. He knew how to do the strategic work necessary to find a way through bureaucracy without losing one's drive or goal. He, too, was unstoppable.

If they discerned with me that I was called to the priesthood, it meant a series of leave-takings: I would leave Trinity, the parish I loved, for a year and intern in another church. I would leave my home in Santa Barbara for three years of seminary, and then a job elsewhere in the diocese. I would leave writing, at least for a while, a profession I had practiced for twenty years. And my marriage. What was to become of that? Vincent said to me the day we chose the committee, "I married a writer, not a priest."

The discernment committee held our first sessions in the fall of 1995. We met for the first time at my house on a Saturday morning around my grandmother's dining-room table. Mark Asman, in his ubiquitous clericals, arrived and explained that this would be his last time with us; he was only here to give us the diocesan requirements for discernment committees. He seemed nervous, and we all felt his tension. He seemed to want to get it right, but none of us knew what "right" was. But just before he left, he seemed to relax and he said, with a small rueful smile, "I envy you this work." As soon as he was out the door, we settled in. Ed asked each of us to respond to the question, How do you hear the Holy Spirit in your life? After a long silence, Mark Benson replied, "I'm racking my brain."

They asked me, at the end of that session, why I thought I needed to be a priest.

"You've been an effective lay leader," Ed said. "Is it necessary for you to be ordained?"

After our first meeting, we rotated from one of our houses to another, like an itinerant circus.

In October, we met at Mark Benson's house. Blue lobelia spilled from planters on his deck, David Austin roses on the slope below. He served bread with bits of chocolate inside. Before beginning the silence, he read from T. S. Eliot's "Little Gidding" with its lines:

> We only live, only suspire
> Consumed by either fire or fire.

He placed the book on the table. Silence fell over us. My monkey brain yammered: Did I turn off the water kettle at home? Is the Allstate bill due today? It was like listening to short-wave radio.

In the silence of the others, I gradually found my footing. In my mind's eye, I saw a stone falling slowly down through clear green water toward a sandy floor. I felt that I could almost see something shaping itself in and among us—like the part of an island hidden under water.

Ed broke the silence. "What is a priest?" he asked.

No one said anything for a minute.

"When Phil was dying, he was in the hospital where I worked," Mark said. "I knew a lot of people in that hospital, but the only time I broke down was when a priest came to visit."

"When I worked for Hospice," Ann Jaqua said, "I had to put together a panel on death and dying and when I went looking for a priest to ask, I have to say, there wasn't one I felt comfortable with."

We ended that session without a clear understanding of what a priest was. We knew how priests had failed us and when they had not, but we were still unclear about what a priest actually was. What was the difference, Ann asked, between a minister and a priest? We invited Mark Asman to come to the next meeting.

In November, the discernment committee met at Ann's house. It's a white two-story cube on a cliff overlooking the sea, like the houses on Corfu, all white and blue. She served tea in thin china cups on a white linen tablecloth. A white orchid bloomed in a celadon pot. The sea had been high the day before, but was now calm. We looked out from her second-story living room onto green, glassy waves. The waves made it easier to sit in silence; their movement lent us a hand.

Mark Asman said, "A priest leads the community. A priest's job is liturgical and sacramental. The other things priests do—administration and teaching—can be done by others but the priest is in the vital role of mediator. The priest in liturgy should help point the community in the direction of God, and keep the liturgy alive rather than make it a museum piece. What gives it legitimacy is the trust relationship built up with the community and what the community invests in it. Then, in some objective way, God, who is always present, becomes more and more transparent."

"Do you agree with that?" Mark Benson asked.

"Yes," I said. I was moved by Mark Asman's words. "But I would add that priesthood feels more to me like a container," I said. "More like a container for a community of faith. A way of helping to balance the whole, and keep it centered without interfering in its course."

"Well," Mark Asman said. "We've got round, and container-like, and we've got, well, we've got standing upright, and. . . . I think we have a female version of priesthood and a male version of priesthood."

At the beginning of the church season of Advent, in early December, we met at Ed's house. We sat outside on his patio under an almost too-warm sun between blooming roses and striking orange birds-of-paradise. It didn't feel like Advent. We asked Mark Benson to read Eliot's poem again and that last line, "Consumed by either fire or fire."

Ann said she wanted to check in as to how our lives were going. "I am waiting," she said. "In Advent, I usually feel as if I were waiting for something."

"I'm waiting too," Ed said. "We haven't bought a tree this year because we're going to our son's house for Christmas."

"I'm waiting," Mark Benson said. "Philip died three years ago. We used to celebrate a big Christmas, so there are things that I won't take out this Christmas. It will be a different Christmas than it was."

Elizabeth said, "This is the second Christmas without Dan. Last year I went to Patrick's house in North Carolina; this year I'll stay here. It is different now, the terrible loneliness has changed."

I could see that because of these hours in silence together, our sadness and pain, the simple burden of living, was beginning to show itself. And because we were taking time to do it, we were each getting the chance to examine our lives, how we chose between the fire and the fire.

"It was as if," Ann Jaqua said later, "by focusing on you, we each got a reflection back."

Later that day, Ed asked me about Vincent. How was he doing in regard to the thoughts about ordination? And what about writing? It seemed to him that writing was so central to my life, how was I going to resolve what might be a conflict between the demands of the two? I came away feeling the time we spent together as muscular, like Jacob's bout with the angel.

A few days later, I heard a story about a group of men who were in prison. They were part of the more than ten thousand political prisoners in this particular country's particular jails. It was Sunday and they wanted to celebrate communion but they had no wine, no bread, no cup, no priest.

"We have no bread, not even water to use as wine," their leader said to them. "But we will act as though we do."

And so he began to lead them in the communion service from the Book of Common Prayer that he had memorized over many years of attending church. When he got to the words of Jesus that are said during the Eucharist prayer, he turned to the man standing next to him, held out his empty hands, and said, "This is my body, which is given for you."

And so they went around the circle, one by one, each man turning to the next one, opening his palms, and saying, "This is my body, given for you."

As our discernment meetings continued, I could see that the Eucharist, with its hidden meanings and mysteries, was at the heart of the matter. On the face of it, the bread, at least, was nothing more than a little fish-food wafer. (Ann Jaqua's grandson, Nicolas, said to her after he received communion for the first time, "Nana, I ate that church chip.") But as I went to church, served the chalice, watched people standing in line to receive, I could see that this central ritual to liturgical churches held within it the image of being fed, of calling forth the unending feast, where there is always enough, nothing is wasted, and no one, not even one, is excluded.

The priest at the altar is said to be presiding. Presiding contains a curious blend of verbs: collecting the energy of the community as one "collects" a horse; weaving, as a woman sits at a loom finding the threads that work with one another to make a pattern; containing, shaping what is present and available—and all of this with a sure sense that the end, the purpose of presiding, is never to dominate but to liberate. The Eucharist is meant to call out of us our own capacity to be sacraments, one for the other. As St. Augustine wrote in a sermon to newly baptized

Christians, "You are the Body of Christ and its members. . . . It is your own mystery that is placed on the Lord's table. And it is to what you are that you reply Amen."

I could see this but I did not know it until several years later when I finally served the bread myself.

On the last Sunday in April, I served the chalice at communion for the first time since Kit died. I saw the face of a woman who was new to the congregation; she worked in a travel store. (Her partner was a sharp-witted, dark-haired woman who was leaving the Roman Catholic Church to join ours.) She looked right back at me. One by one, I served them: John, who held his adopted daughter from China; Sage, who was recovering from an accident; Carol, a Guggenheim scholar who was writing an account of the Italian working poor in thirteenth-century Bologna; a little boy with red hair so pale it was like a new peach, who opened up his hand and reached for the chalice and then smiled at me as if he were the sun. I looked in their eyes, and they looked back, and for a moment we were a part of a wide glittering web of giving and receiving, what Ann Jaqua called a gift exchange. I rocked back on my heels; I was almost unable to move except that moving was part of it. Moving was at its core.

And yet even in the midst of this community, even after seven years, even as I imagined priesthood, I was like my friend Harriet, who told me about a Sunday when she was listening to a banal sermon at the National Cathedral in Washington. The priest asked, in unctuous tones, Now what do you really want for Christmas this year? Harriet said, "I nearly rose from my pew. I was gathering myself up until I looked over at my sister who was giving me That Look, and I sat back down, but what I wanted to do was stand up and call out, 'I would like to really believe in the resurrection.' "

2

I am six. Kit is twelve. He's broken his leg skiing, practicing for a race. He is my captive while he recovers, leg in a giant white cast, aluminum crutches with foam padding taped on the arm-rests. He crutches around and I invent games: tag and hide-and-seek are mainstays but also games based on books my mother reads to me. One involves hidden treasure and trolls under a bridge. Our dad is about to disappear. I can feel him leaving. Kit knows what it is about; I do not. I believe that if I simply do not ask about him, but take it all in stride—fathers come, fathers go—everything will return to normal. Meanwhile, I have my one brother to myself. Kit usually allows me to tag along to the older kids' games and then ignores me, but right now, he is all mine. And in the midst of one game of tag, when he laughs out loud as I run around, my braids flying, I see in his face that he is happy here with me, that he is enjoying this time alone with me as much as I am with him, and I can hardly contain my joy.

In February, when Kit was still able to drive, Vincent and I visited him and his partner, Rande, for a few days. We drove around in his Bronco on the backroads of southern New Mexico, near his hometown of Polvadera, and took pictures of each other in a drywash called San Lorenzo Canyon. The dogs, Here Boy and Rita, climbed up and down on red rock. Rande and I swam in a hot spring. Kit's son, Robert, and his girlfriend, Michele, met us in Water Canyon, where snow still lay deep under the aspens. We hiked around, dousing each other with snowballs, but in the late afternoon I looked over and saw my brother's face creased with pain. He could barely make it back up the hill to the car.

We planned excursions and revised them. One day we drove south on the interstate and then took a road into the town of Monticello where an adobe church with a white bell tower lit inside with only votives faced the town square.

We drove up Lost Canyon along a narrow river. On the way, we passed a truck buried to its bed in the sand.

"What year is that?" Vincent asked Kit.

"Nineteen forty-five," Kit replied.

When we got to an impassable piece of the road, I said to Kit, "Go that way. Ford the river, and then up, over that other bank."

"Okay," he said, turning the wheel.

"You are the only person he listens to," said Rande, laughing, as she handed me a Swiss cheese and green chili sandwich.

Rock walls stained with desert varnish, adobe ruins, and, out on the highway, a snow storm hit, blowing white. As we drove back toward town, we could see in the distance the Magdalena Range, the flat wide plain of San Agustin, and on it huge white disks like giant morning glories facing the distant sky: the Very Large Array, fourteen radio telescopes trained on the far reaches of the universe where the atoms from the Big Bang still race outward, sending information back from the past.

That evening Kit said he wanted to take us out to the Bosque del Apache, a bird refuge, a wetlands sanctuary salvaged from cattle ranches. The Bosque is a home to red-winged blackbirds, mallard ducks, red-tailed hawks, and a way station for many migratory birds. Thousands of snow geese, Canada geese, and sandhill cranes winter there, as well as six whooping cranes. We drove out to a viewing platform set in one of the farther ponds to watch the sandhill cranes come in to land. Among the largest of the crane family, sandhills stand as tall as four feet. Their wing spans reach seven feet.

I leaned against the platform railing and Kit's elbow. We saw nothing at first. Then, as the sun was setting, tall figures appeared in the sky, far off, silent at first and then crying out, a bird chant: *ga-roo-a, ga-roo-a.* I counted a hundred and stopped counting. As they came nearer, they began to fall feet first toward the shallow water. I held my breath. They were only a foot above the surface when they shot out their wings and came to a standstill in the air. Then they floated to the water, like ballerinas, and settled in to feed.

Before he got so sick he couldn't work, Kit walked all over the state surveying the Rio Grande basin for the Bureau of Land Management.

Kit knew New Mexico. He loved the rivers in the north; the orchards fed by each village's *acequia madre;* and the ruins of an Anasazi village at Chaco Canyon dating from 1030, where the Great Kiva, the round ceremonial house, measures one hundred feet across. At Chaco four straight roads from the four directions lead into the main pueblo. Thirty feet wide, made of packed earth or bedrock, cut through low hills, with masonry stairs and masonry ramps over minor cliff edges and ravines filled in, they were built before the Anasazi had wheels, a compass, surveying instruments, or the words for them. On a roof in a shallow cave is painted a red sliver of a sun, dated to 1054, the year of a supernova.

In order to survey, Kit said, you always have to have two points. In a photo, he leans over his tripod looking through the scope, high above Otowi Bridge in northern New Mexico, sighting a distant point on the other side of the river. Below him are mesas dotted with piñon trees, a river gorge, a line of blue mesas, and beyond them nothing but a line of clouds in the sky. He marched through salt cedar and tamarisk, the bosque thick with snakes, finding the landmarks that aligned with each other. He could map anything. I thought of him then as making sense of geography.

His life on the face of it was not successful. He was a drinking alcoholic; he took the sixties on the chin. Our dad, who had left us for a year—to recover from his own alcoholism—and then returned, kept trying to talk to him about the drinking, but Kit didn't listen. I was babysitting his first child one night when men in dark coats arrived at the door with Kit, and his wife Kathy, and a search warrant. "FBI," they said to me, just like the movies, and began digging with shovels in the backyard, searching, we found out later, for marijuana smuggled over the border from Mexico. Kit was found innocent of the charges after a desperate court battle during which officials of the government lied under oath so often that they first astonished and then enraged our dad, a lawyer, who ended up distrusting the government and turned against the war in Vietnam.

Kit and Kathy moved to California and rented a houseboat across the pier from Alan Watts, the east west philosopher, in Sausalito. They had a second son, the two boys in diapers. I visited and stood on the dock watching journalists climb the gangway to learn about Zen.

When Kit and Kathy broke up, our parents took in the boys. The years went by and the children remained with their grandparents. Kit complained about the arrangement, said he wanted the boys back, but never did anything serious about it.

His second wife, Angel, a Zuni Native American, drowned on a cold morning. After Angel's death, Kit found work as a handyman and gardener for a couple who lived in a big house near Albuquerque. The man was a physicist who'd worked at Los Alamos; he'd been bruised and hardened by weapons research. His young wife was experimenting with pottery. Kit grieved for Angel and drank. I would visit once a year and stand against a wall, trying to speak the words that would release him.

He met Rande Brown when my mother placed an ad in the newspaper for a housesitter. She and my father were taking the boys to Ireland for the summer. Rande had just been released from a mental ward with someone else's clothing and a quarter. She called the number in the ad. Kit met the new housesitter when he came over to say goodbye to the boys.

Together, they renovated a burned-out adobe in Polvadera. He built a living room with vigas of pine, brick floors, and plastered walls that were light brown, like the outside of an egg. When Rande stayed up too late, drank too much coffee, and veered into mania, he took her to the hospital and waited for her to come out. When he applied for the surveyor's job and got it, she sang to him. She cooked and grew gourd vines and string beans and worked as a greenhouse gardener. They were veterans of everything. When they fought too hard and too dirty, a year before he was diagnosed with cancer, he said, "Let's quit drinking together."

When asked to give a toast once to the things he loved, he replied, "Home-grown tomatoes, enduring tunes, and true love."

He taught me about familial love. It was a wisdom he learned the hard way. He embodied a certain kind of discernment. He would not bend reality to suit his will, but instead took things exactly as they came to him. The result was that the pain and suffering he went through in his life had to be worked in him, had to come to a shape inside him that made sense to *him*. That was how he came to know so much about love, and to pass it on. His love for me was specific, precise, and practical. "New Mexico misses you," he wrote on the back of a photograph of a sunset he had taken that he sent as a postcard. For Christmas he sent me ristras, chains of red chili, to hang outside my door and remind me of the place we grew up in. He praised Vincent, and my good judgment in marrying him. He praised my work and my dreams. I knew from way back that I could trust him. He was my other point.

3

Nave, apse, sanctuary, crossing—I could recite the parts of a church as a prayer. Alb, chasuble, stole, surplice, cassock—beads on a rosary. Corporal, purificator, chalice, paten, host. Old, specific words like imprints of leaves in stone carrying the language of the past.

When Mark Asman had been at Trinity only a few months, he preached a sermon about how the heart in Hebrew scripture was not only the place of feeling but also the seat of access to everything in the self: the body, the mind, feelings. The heart is like a room available to every part of the self, to which nothing is hidden in shadow.

During his first six months at Trinity he was like a thoroughbred returning to the track, easily spooked but filled with energy. He sneaked into hospital recovery rooms to anoint the sick, paraded newly baptized babies down the church aisle, and preached about how much God loves us. He flirted shamelessly with elderly women and raised large sums of money for a city-ordered earthquake retrofit of the church and parish hall. "I'm just a whore for Jesus," he sighed one evening as he lowered himself into his convertible Saab to drive out to a wealthy suburb to extract yet another pledge.

He drew little charts for where people serving at the altar were to stand during the big festival services. He held rehearsals. He gave a tour of the sacristy, formerly a place where only those designated to serve at the altar were welcome, and pulled out a particularly startling gold chasuble (the robe worn by priests when celebrating the Eucharist). He said, "Don't you think this would look good with fishnet stockings?"

He had a beautiful chanting voice. His office was papered in stacks of letters, financial reports, and gifts from the Sunday school children (who were beginning to climb in numbers). "Hang onto your garter belts," was a favorite expression.

Ordained to the priesthood at twenty-five, he left active ministry at thirty-two, returning after ten years to an interim post at Trinity. When the vestry deliberated over whether to "call" Mark as our permanent rector, he told us that he was a priest "who was also a gay man." Compressed into this statement was an attempt to change his sexual orientation by healing prayer, that ten-year sabbatical from active priesthood during which he came out to himself and worked for, among other places, the March of Dimes as a telephone solicitor and I. Magnin clothing company, and finally returned to full-time ministry.

Now the vestry faced an interesting dilemma: while its members knew Mark was gay, he had not come out to the parish as a whole. He had not ducked any private questions from parishioners, but there had been few of those. Work had been done on the subject of human sexuality at Trinity: educational forums held in the fall of 1995 explored sexuality and repression in the church, the ordination of homosexuals, and even a role-play about same-gender marriage. On the national scene that year, in a surprise move, a group of Episcopal bishops brought charges of heresy against a retired bishop, Walter Righter, for ordaining an openly gay man; his would be the first trial of a bishop for heresy since 1923. As our vestry pondered its own predicament, Righter's trial was set to begin in an ecclesiastical court. It was as if our church was a miniature, or a hologram, of a larger play being acted out on a larger stage.

.   .   .

I was walking to my car after the Thursday-night service, when Mark came out the door and matched his stride to mine.

"I need to talk to a few folks to get a bead on something," he said. "Do you think you can manage a meeting, a small one?"

I said I thought I could, and we set the meeting for the next Monday night at my house.

Steve Gibson, the senior warden of the vestry, arrived early. A partner at a funeral home in Santa Barbara, a moderate Republican, and the father of Nathan, two years old, Steve was the vestry member who urged the vestry forward, last August, to hire a gay man as the church's priest, even as the larger church was in bitter disagreement over the issue and no one could predict what it would cost.

In a few minutes I heard heavy footsteps on the front porch and Mark and George Barrett arrived. George was a retired bishop, as tall as Mark, and had an aristocratic bearing. In 1975, after much prayer and conversation, George ordained four women to the priesthood in Washington, when it was still "illegal" in the church, believing as he wrote later that "women's liberation is implicit in the Christian gospel." (The church leadership finally voted to ordain women as priests at its convention in 1976.) George called or wrote to each woman on the anniversary of her ordination every year. He answered every letter sent to him regarding the ordinations, especially those who disagreed with his action because as he said, "My greatest temptation was the spiritual pride that puts others down as less intelligent and far more prejudiced than oneself."

When he was eighty-five, his daughter said, he came to visit her in St. Paul, Minnesota, while a fair was in town and insisted that they go out so he could test the rides. Finding a particularly scary one, he handed Myra his glasses and climbed on.

"I stood there watching 'Rollerball' or whatever it was called rise straight up into the sky with my eighty-five-year-old father's glasses in my hand, praying he would not have a stroke," Myra said. "When he got off, I asked him how it was. 'Too tame,' he replied."

When he was first consecrated bishop, the microphone began screeching as he stood up to preach. "Your cross, sir," said one of the priests present, "is causing static."

"This won't be the last time," murmured one of his friends.

George embodied discernment, as did Kit. If Kit fought to find the truth inside him, George knew how to let things go. By ordaining the women in Washington, he let go of a certain kind of respectibility in the church, but without flamboyance or self-indulgence. It started earlier in his life and ministry. When he became Bishop of Rochester, in the early sixties, the city was soon to be in the midst of race riots. Black protesters demanded change from Eastman Kodak, and George helped to hire Saul Alinksy, the community organizer, to work in the neighborhoods and bolster the strength of the black community. He resigned as bishop in 1969, divorced his wife, and married his present wife, Bettina, a poet and painter. He and Bettina left Rochester, and moved to San Francisco where, with a small group of people, including the widow of Bishop Pike, he discerned his next move. He ended up directing Planned Parenthood in Santa Barbara. George let go of a career in the church to start something new. I once saw George getting ready to cross the street as I was driving to church. I waved and motioned for him to cross in front of me. He motioned back, to roll down my window.

"I'll cross the street when I'm ready," he growled and, grinning, waved me on.

He would, eventually, show us how to let everything go.

. . .

Ann Jaqua rushed in, late, and sat down. Mark began, "At our vestry meeting in April this year, the human sexuality committee brought a suggestion to the vestry that we consider blessing same-sex unions at Trinity." He cleared his throat. "The parish is aware of this report, but nothing has been said publicly about my sexuality.

"I need to have your various opinions about what my options are," Mark continued, resting his chin on his hand.

"You are the rector of the parish," George snorted. "If you want to keep your private life private, you certainly may."

"I agree," Ann said. "You have the right to have a private life. It is really nobody's business. It's beside the point. I mean, no one asks a heterosexual rector to talk about his private sexual life."

"I think you have to tell them," said Stephen. "The problem now is that some people, like the vestry, know and some people don't. That creates an in crowd. It's not healthy for the parish."

"The question is how," Ann said.

"The question is when," I said.

"If you decide, or we decide together, to bless same-sex relationships then you really must tell the parish, I think," Ann said. "It can't be something that is found out accidentally."

"I'm with you but spell out to me why," Mark said.

"This is basically intuitive," Ann replied and then grinned at Mark.

"Oh, great," he said.

"It goes something like this," she continued. "If you make a stand about homosexual unions and don't publicly state that you are a homosexual, it will feel weird. If I, for one, were 'to find out about you' after you'd made a stand, and other than by you telling us, I would feel betrayed."

"I am not at all sure we should bless same-sex unions at Trinity," Stephen said. "The rest of you are way ahead of me on this score."

"You and a lot of other people in the parish," Mark said. "We're all going to have to spend a lot of time on this."

It was late and we decided to quit for now, to pray, and think, and talk more. I felt anxious after the meeting; I couldn't figure out how we were going to move from one place to another. We were a church community, for better or for worse, not a political community. I couldn't force people to agree with me, nor did I want to. There were elderly women and young fathers and people at Trinity who were like Stephen. There were people who didn't want to know that Mark was gay. There were many gay priests in the Episcopal church but almost all of them were closeted, even in Los Angeles. Trinity had no real models for how to bring a priest out.

I figured I'd pray about it. I didn't really understand prayer. But I'd been taking advice on prayer from my mother, who likes Agnes Sanford, an Episcopal healer and mystic from the thirties. Sanford's basic idea was that you did all you could to imagine a good outcome for something, whatever your "good" was, and you did the hard work necessary to imagine it in all its detail and then you said, "Or thy will." Thus you were an active participant. (I had always been wary of the "surrender to God" school of prayer, which seems to make one more passive than is necessary in a relationship with a being that doesn't seem to encourage or desire passivity.) But at the end of all that imagining of good, you knew that you didn't have the whole picture, so you then turned it over.

So I prayed. I imagined a Trinity where Mark was standing in the pulpit and people in the pews were attentive but not rigid. I imagined a Trinity where everyone knew that Mark was gay. Then I imagined those people who came to us as prayer ministers, with hidden fears and dreads and illnesses and addictions, added in my own hidden anxiety and depression and envy, and I imagined some of that "out of the closet," too. I imagined us all less cleaned up and more real sitting in the pews, hoping that

God would breathe on us today. You cannot create love, said a poet, but you can create the conditions for love. I thought of us all sitting there with our fears and sins sitting right alongside us, as fierce beasts, wishing to be healed. Then I said, "Or thy will."

In a few days, I got a phone call from Stephen.

"I want to talk to you about what I have been thinking," he said.

"Okay," I replied, putting down my tea.

"When I got home from the meeting, I went in to see Nathan in his crib. He was asleep. It suddenly occurred to me, what if Nathan should grow up to be gay? I don't want him to because I want grandchildren but if he did, then what?"

"Yep," I replied.

"He's my son," Stephen said. "If he is gay, I want the world to be a better place for him.

"And I don't want the church to withhold any sacrament from my son."

I held my breath.

"Including," Stephen said, sighing, "the sacrament of marriage."

"Thank you," I replied.

"Oh, God," Stephen said, "I'm becoming a liberal."

4

I flew from LAX into Albuquerque, walked past the glass cases containing plates with coyotes painted on them and turquoise necklaces (feeling at once at home in New Mexico and embarrassed by its tourist kitsch), rented a car, and drove south. Polvadera is eighty miles from Albuquerque in another world from Santa Fe and Taos. It boasts a post office and what Kit and I called the world's largest junkyard. It's a place people go to hide; few of Kit's friends had listed phone numbers.

I checked into the Holiday Inn Express in nearby Socorro and drove over to my brother's house, past block after block of wrecked Chevies and Ford pick-ups, broken windshields gleaming in the weak March sun. In New Mexico in the spring, a steady wind blows from the west. When we were kids we imagined that at least some of the Grand Canyon would eventually end up in our backyard. Kit once came home from college and wrote "D-u-s-t" with his fingertip on the brick floor of his bedroom. I made a right and I was on a dirt road. I like the feel of dirt under the wheels of a car; it feels more welcoming than pavement. I saw Kit and Rande's stockade fence, a series of thin poles with bark still on them wired together, and Rande's gourd vine hanging over it. The Bronco that Kit couldn't drive anymore sat in the driveway.

I walked around the corner of the adobe house and into Kit's yard. The dogs barked from inside. I heard Kit's voice, weak, telling Here Boy to relax. I opened the screen door and saw my brother seated on the couch pushing his hands against the cushions like an old man trying to get up. I made it over to him before he could stand and he wrapped his arms around me and said, "Baby sister. How was your trip?"

I told him it was fine. Rande offered me some tea and toast and then she packed up her camping gear to take off for two days. We'd settled into a routine. I arrive each week on Sunday night and leave on Tuesday evening. My friend Anne Strasburg thought of this plan after praying for me and Kit, then falling asleep. It had come to her on waking, all of a piece.

I'd live in New Mexico for two days, in dust and poverty and illness, and then come home, driving back late on Highway 101, in the wet California air, past Volvo and Mercedes dealers and neat green lawns. I felt as if the flights basted time and space together with loose ragged threads. I did not know how long it would last.

People say their faith is tested during such times, but I am not sure I had much faith to test. I knew what I did not believe in: that God was holding Kit in his hands (and the whole world, etc.), or that Kit was going on to eternal life or that Kit's suffering and mine were for some greater good. Those statements seemed like so many platitudes to me or at least none of them helped me, none of them gave me a shred of solace. None of them carried weight. I don't know what I believed in. This was beyond anything I had had to endure, beyond anything I could will or imagine. My only brother was suffering, turning into skin and bones. Some part of me knew he was dying. I had to go to New Mexico every week to help Rande and find my brother, hear his words, his thoughts, or only be in the room with him, his hands, his face, his shirt, his shoes. Hold on to each and every last bit of him. One thing I knew: other people were praying for Kit and for me. The monks at Mt. Calvary Monastery in Santa Barbara had told me they were praying for us at matins, at diurnum, at vespers; the women who met on Friday morning at Trinity were praying for us as they prayed for everyone on the church "prayer list." Anne

Strasburg had prayed for me. I could not pray myself, or at least I could not formulate words or wishes. If I sat still long enough to pray, I found only a room filled with a long scream. I finally began to see that I was living on other people's prayers, as if they were bread and water. Sometimes during the day, around noon, I would feel a little lift, and I finally connected it to the brothers in their chapel, in their white hooded habits, saying out loud, "For Kit Gallagher, who has cancer, and Nora, his sister." Prayers were what I came to believe in; they were the glue that bound me to the living, and made it possible for me to remain upright and walk.

Later in the day, I walked around the yard behind Kit in his blue bathrobe and slippers to catch him if he fell as he picked up empty beer bottles and plastic sacks that had blown against the fence. His legs were as thin as broom handles.

In the late afternoon, I asked him if he would like to say compline, the service for the close of the day, with its beautiful soft words, "Hide us under the shadow of your wings."

"Yes, I would like that," he replied, closing his eyes.

At the end, I read the prayer from St. Augustine: "Keep watch dear Lord with those who work, or watch, or weep this night, and give your angels charge over those who sleep. Tend the sick, Lord Christ; give rest to the weary, bless the dying, soothe the suffering, pity the afflicted, shield the joyous; and all for your love's sake."

"Shield the joyous," Kit said. "I like that. When you are joyful, you need a shield."

Between us on the chest were my Book of Common Prayer, his *Snow Falling on Cedars,* and bottles of liquid morphine. I watched him sleep.

When he woke up, I got him some grape juice.

"I had a daydream about the Great Kiva at Chaco," he said.

"What was it about?"

"The supporting posts for the kiva are trees. They were probably carried from the Jemez Mountains. No one knows how they carried them. That's a ways. I'd say twenty miles. And the stone walls were so carefully made, all of them must have been stonemasons.

"And as the walls rose higher and higher, the stones for the facade became thinner and thinner," he looked at me, and he grinned, "as thin as cigarette papers."

The door was open to the yard. Outside, the wind was blowing dust to the river. Kit looked straight out the door. I saw nothing there. He lifted his head.

"Look!" he said.

5

I kept saying, "I lost him." As if I had misplaced him. As if it were my fault. I lost him, not "he was lost." Like my glasses or my keys or the socks in the washing machine, Kit was somewhere else and I couldn't find him. I could feel my body looking for him, nerve endings reaching out. It felt as if he were nearby, as if in the next room. And if I only had the wherewithal, I would find him. Years after he died, I had a dream that he had been living in Santa Barbara the whole time and I hadn't known it.

As April turned to May, I saw that I was living in a different rhythm, forced on me by grief. I simply could not do all the things I normally did. I could not jump from one task to the next. I couldn't sit in long meetings. I couldn't be with crowds. I inhabited a world that was small, and slow.

I came to see that this small slow world had its own secrets, as if it were a universe running just parallel to the one we normally inhabit. It had the drunk who had held hands with Mark at the Thursday Eucharist, it had the red-tailed hawk, and it had Kit's body. It had broken bits and discarded memories. It had a Folger's coffee can I had seen on a window sill in Santa Fe, stuffed with geraniums. It had memories of Kit's and my childhood, a trip we took as children into the wilderness of northern New Mexico where we passed blind windowless churches called *moradas*. Pine needles coated with rain. It was like a garage sale.

A spiritual director told me once that God is found on the

edge of things, in the margins. About a drunk who sleeps on Trinity's porch he said, "You can ask him not to drink on the porch but you can't ask him to leave. He lives in the part that makes the church uncomfortable and that's where Jesus lives."

I was living there, too.

In this world, I slept and ate. I had dreams. I knew that there was something hidden in the things that were giving me solace and those that were not. There was nothing coherent about them, no thought that encompassed all of the things together or made them coalesce; I just experienced various moments more acutely, and to some I responded better than others, or more completely. To some experiences—the coffee hour at church, a business meeting—I simply could not acquiesce. I had been stripped of the ability to endure small talk and boredom; or rather, I began to see, I had lost whole sections of the self that endured those things.

I decided to spend a night at the monastery, to fall into the arms of the monks. I drove past Santa Barbara's old mission, and up winding mountain roads. I parked and walked along the low wall that protects the monastery against a long drop into Rattlesnake Canyon. The ceiling of the portal was painted dark blue with gold stars.

Brother Robert, the prior of the monastery, greeted me at the door, took my hand, and walked me down to the chapel without speaking. I began to cry, and he held my hand tighter. At the vespers service he prayed, "For the soul of Kit."

Ann Jaqua arrived and we shared a room with two narrow beds covered in white chenille and a window that slid open onto the garden. Outside, in the dark, an owl called. After dinner and compline, when the monks entered what is called the Great Silence, Ann and I whispered together in the dark. She'd just returned from Hawaii, and she told me about a tree she saw there—one of the few native plants remaining on Maui. It was an acacia, living in a cloud forest. Its leaves were shaped like sickles and set in whirls around the branches. Her guide pointed out that the leaves were made to collect vapor from the clouds that hung overhead and then direct the droplets into its base and thus to the roots of the tree.

"It all fit so perfectly together. Something about it made me cry," she said. "I have been haunted by it ever since. I realized when I returned that there was no place where I felt so perfectly adapted. I wasn't in relationship with the natural world. I was an intruder everywhere I went."

I was reminded of an afternoon I spent on a beach at Pt. Reyes, in northern California. I walked behind a largely self-taught naturalist who was like a very well-educated twelve-year-old. With her big glasses, her long skinny legs, her knobby knees, her cargo shorts stuffed with books, carrying her scope, she led us down Drake's Beach, scooping up sand at the water's edge. With one palm cupped around the greenish gooey sand, she sifted through it with her long fingers. A shell emerged, shaped like a miniature armadillo.

"Look! Mole crab," she cried. Gently brushing sand off the crab's shell, she showed us the little feelers above its head used to filter detritus from the ocean at the edge of the surf, the egg cavities on the underside sheltering orange eggs the size of new peas, the perfect digging forked legs at the rear. She placed the crab back down at the edge of the surf, and we watched as the crab dug herself in, disappearing in a few seconds, the only sign of her a slight wrinkle in the sand. Shorebirds can read the sand for those bumps; their bills are suited to digging and scooping and have sensitive pads on the ends to detect the crabs.

"The natural world fits together," Ann said. "It's so intricate. It's one of those things that exceeds us in intelligence, freedom, and purpose. It can't be pinned down."

Rabbi Abraham Heschel says, when we reach the shores of

reason, we hear the waves of the ineffable beating against the sand. As I sat with Ann in our room I heard the owl outside; I heard that Hawaiian tree and the mole crab, each of them singing in my ears.

When I returned from the monastery, the world's concerns were writ large. The "heresy trial," the trial of Bishop Walter Righter, had begun earlier in the spring. Any day now, a decision would come down. When the trial had first convened, in March, Karen Armstrong, author of *A History of God,* wrote in the *New York Times,* "History shows that heresy trials are largely fueled by a church's anxiety over challenges to its authority and social change."

The human sexuality committee was getting ready to meet again. Various members said they thought the fall was a good time to talk about same-sex blessings. Some people, including me, were worried about the timing. Fall is the traditional time for stewardship in the church, for collecting from its members the pledged dollars that will keep it running and, most important, pay the priest's salary for the next year. People might not say anything out loud, but they could vote with their pocketbooks. How many members might we lose outright? We were growing, but we weren't a large church yet; we still relied on our endowment from the people-rich past to fill in budget gaps. What about the young families just starting to come in the door?

But Ed Potts urged action. He said to a few of us, "Is it right to ask, concerning justice questions, 'Why should we do it now?' rather than 'Why should we *not* do it now?' "

On May 15, the court on the Righter case acted. "There is no core doctrine prohibiting the ordination of a noncelibate homosexual person living in a faithful and committed sexual relationship with a person of the same sex. There is no discipline of the church prohibiting the ordination of a noncelibate person living in a committed relationship with a person of the same sex," read the Bishop of Delaware. In the pew in front of him,

Walter Righter held his wife's hand and bowed his head. One huge hurdle was crossed; Mark Asman was now "safer." The court, however, had said nothing about the church blessing same-sex relationships. This was not the issue before it. If Trinity became a place where blessings took place, what would happen to us, to Mark?

The human sexuality committee met in June and proposed to the vestry that Mark preach a sermon in late September to open the conversation, followed by a series of forums that would address such things as the Bible and homosexuality, fears about welcoming gay couples ("becoming a gay church"), and what a blessing might actually look like.

The vestry met in August and approved the proposal. The question of the contents of the sermon were left to Mark. Now the pressure was really on. One Sunday afternoon, Mark, Anne Howard, Ann Jaqua, Stephen, and I sat in the parish hall and talked it over. We seemed to have been through every possible scenario. No one liked the idea of Mark "coming out in the pulpit," but none of us could think of another way to tell everyone, all at once, so it would be over and we could go on to other things.

Finally, someone suggested that Mark write a letter to the parish, and mail it the week preceding the sermon. Stephen said the vestry could write a letter, too, to support Mark, and explain our history together. "And then," said Ann Jaqua, "you could say whatever you want to say in the sermon, but your coming out need not be its whole purpose." It seemed suddenly simple.

Stephen and I worked together on the letter from the vestry: "To everything there is a season," Stephen began. ". . .[T]hese seasons belong to God, and they are the time frame of the church. . . . Sometimes this time of God brings us into conflict with the world. It calls us to take a stand, to change, sometimes to take unpopular, even dangerous positions. . . .

"As a vestry," Stephen continued, in the third paragraph, "we hope all of you are aware of the steps we are beginning to take at Trinity to become a more open and affirming church to our gay brothers and sisters. We want Trinity to be an open and affirming church because we are a family, because we are striving to accept one another without reservation, and because we have called Mark, a priest who happens to be a gay man, as our rector."

There it was. When I worked as a journalist, we called it burying the lead.

In the library, Mark sat alone with a yellow legal tablet and a pencil. He wrote his letter without consulting anyone except George Barrett. Then he began on the sermon. Every hour or so, a page of Mark's scrawled handwriting fell from my fax machine. The gospel for Sunday, September 22, was Matthew 20: 1–16 about the vineyard owner and his laborers. It has a famous refrain, "And the last shall be first and the first shall be last."

He finished the sermon at 7:00 p.m., faxed me the last page, and went home to nap.

The letters were both mailed on the morning of Monday, September 16, a saint's day for Ninian, Bishop of Galloway, who in the fourth or early fifth century seems to have converted a number of Scottish Picts to Christianity. The Picts were not known for their pleasant reception to foreigners, so Ninian must have been not only persuasive but brave. I liked the connection.

I received Mark's letter the next day. "Dear Friends," he wrote,

> I would like to tell you a story about someone I know. This story is about a young man who grew up in a very average family and like all of us, worked at knowing he was loved by family, friends, and God. While he was growing up, and even into his adulthood, he knew there was something about himself that was different. . . . His

sexuality was different and he could not accept it. . . . As he grew into his thirties he began to recognize that the energy spent denying this part of his life was making him profoundly unhappy. This seemed strange given the loving God he had come to know. So he decided to do something about this sadness. He decided to try accepting his differentness. He decided to accept his homosexuality. This act of acceptance brought him peace and wholeness.

Why have I told you this story? Because it is my story.

Mark then explained why the parish needed to know this information. He outlined the human sexuality committee's process and then he wrote, "What became clear to me and the vestry was that in order for me to preach about same-sex blessings as an issue of justice you needed to know that this was also a personal issue for me. To do anything less would be dishonest. At this point in our growth as a community, we all need to have the same information."

He proposed that the parish take the rest of the year to talk over same-sex blessings, in various forums organized by the human sexuality committee, and he urged people to talk to him privately. And at the end, he wrote out a prayer from the Book of Common Prayer, which read in part, "O God of unchangeable power and eternal light: Look favorably on your whole Church, that wonderful and sacred mystery . . . let the whole world see and know that things which were cast down are being raised up, and things which had grown old are being made new. . . ."

Sunday, September 22, the seventeenth Sunday after Pentecost, was bright and clear, the midstream of Indian summer in Santa

Barbara. By 9:45, the church was packed for the ten o'clock service.

"If the church welcomes lesbian women and gay men to the table then the church needs to be committed to doing everything it can to sustain us in our journey of faith, as it does for everyone. . . ." Mark preached. "How can the church say you can have this sacrament, the sacrament of baptism, but not the sacrament of ordination? How can the church say you can be fed by the Eucharist, but your loving committed relationships cannot be blessed and affirmed by the church?" When he was finished, he turned around and walked down the two stairs of the pulpit, across the pavement stones to his chair and sat down.

The service went on, as if nothing had changed.

We said the Nicene Creed. We said the Prayers of the People. We prayed for all people in their daily lives and work, for anyone in danger or sorrow. We said the confession. And then we greeted one another by wishing each other "Peace be with you." There was quite a lot of hugging. And then, at the break between the liturgy of the word and the liturgy of the table, when in many churches various announcements are made, Mark stood up and slowly walked over to face the congregation. He said, "Well, I don't know about you but I've had quite a week," and the whole place burst into applause and then everyone jumped to their feet as if we had been sprung from prison.

In the end, a handful of people left the church; many of them returned within a year.

None of our fears came to pass. Pledges rose. During that fall, in the forums on human sexuality, many gay and straight people told their stories. One rainy night, it was Mark Benson's turn. He told the story of the blessing of his relationship with Philip at All Saints in Pasadena. He said that it really was a story "about how two men were loved by a parish so much that they just had to give a party for the whole place."

He ended his story that night by saying, "We both had grown up in a Christian tradition that finally couldn't have us, and wouldn't hold us as we struggled to understand the mystery of our sexuality, and so just had to let us go, as that tradition has let so many go. But at All Saints we found a safe haven, a community strong enough to take us in and hear us. . . . And so that's why we were so pleased to celebrate with the whole parish, our life together, and our life with them."

Doing the right thing, I saw, takes practice. Our experience with Mark Asman gave us fortitude. As the word spread that Trinity was a parish that walked its talk, more and more people, of all ages and orientations, began coming through the doors. We could see that it was attractive to people to be a brave church, to actually do the work the Gospels proclaimed. And I saw that while I sought completion or wholeness, Trinity was a community that was seeking wholeness, too.

A parishioner from Trinity who was working on a national committee taking a look at church growth was asked how Trinity had become so successful.

"We broke all the rules," she said.

6

The week after Easter, on Tuesday night, I returned from my regular visit to Kit and dreamed that he was riding a horse. His saddle was a wooden box. A nurse carried a balloon. She said, This will help. I ran after him but he was going through a door.

In the morning, I called him. He could hardly hear. I fretted and paced. I drove downtown and met with Ann Jaqua.

Should I get on a plane right away, I asked her. Or should I wait, as I said I would, until Sunday night? What should I do?

She said, "You've staked your life that the next step will be revealed."

Those words penetrated me as if they were made of anointing oil. And it came to me that I was about to take a completely trusting solid step in what I called in shorthand faith but what was actually an accumulation of moments, pieced together to make something beautiful, like those walls at Chaco, sliver of stone by stone.

The next day, I sat in my study and prayed in a jumbled, tangled string of words, then began to edit an essay. It slipped in like a cat, a clear thought without anxiety: "Today." I walked into the house and said to Vincent, "We're leaving tonight." He looked up, closed the cover of his laptop and said, "Fine." I will always remember that it took him one motion.

When we drove south from Albuquerque that night a huge disk floated in the sky above the river. We knew it had to be the moon, but it was so huge, so bright, it looked like the sun. It lit up the towns as we passed them, old adobes and new cinderblock buildings, squares against the low hills, the flat desert. It was midnight when we arrived, but I wanted to see Kit. The lights were on as we drove in. He was sitting up on the couch, his black hair plastered against his forehead the way he used to look as a boy when he had a fever.

"Hello," he said to me, and I saw he was not sure who I was. He tried to stand up, but wavered, and sat back down.

I sat next to him and cuddled up to him.

"I love you," I said.

"Oh, good."

I got up and went into the kitchen for water. Kit whispered to Vincent, "Is she coming back?"

Rande put her hand on Kit's forehead and shook her head.

"Too hot, I think," she said. She wet a cloth and placed it against his skin, then gave him several Tylenol. I pushed back his hair, kissed him on his now cool forehead, kissed Rande, and we drove back to the Motel Six.

At four in the morning, I got up and drove over to his house and sat in the driveway. The house was dark. I watched the stars, then drove back to the hotel and got into bed.

At seven we returned. At noon, the Hospice nurse arrived, a gentle shy man dressed in khakis and a polyester shirt. He introduced himself as Norbert. We had talked to Kit all morning but he had not replied. Norbert leaned over him and spoke loudly into his ear.

"Christopher! Would you like a hospital bed? It would be more comfortable."

"NO!"

"Well, that's clear," he said, sitting back.

.   .   .

I looked up and saw Vincent outside with a group of Kit's friends standing all around him. He had a beer in one hand and a cigarette in the other, necessary props for Polvadera. He was gesturing with the cigarette. The men were leaning toward him, listening.

"Arranging the afternoon," Vincent said, coming into the room. "Though I'm not sure who will be sober."

I walked around picking things up and putting them down. Two silver mint julep cups won by our great-grandfather in a golf tournament in Winnetka. A photo of Kit's sons when they were boys, holding onto our mother's wraparound skirt. My father, holding a "Lawyer of the Year" award from the Bar Association, looking shy and pleased as punch. Dust. A dry red chili. A letter from our cousin Nan. She was back-country skiing in the Cascades and saw the tracks of a lynx.

Leaving Kit with a man who was almost sober, Vincent and I went back to the hotel to nap. I fell into the bed and slept ten minutes and woke up sweating. When we returned, the guy and his girlfriend were playing Scrabble. Kit was fidgeting. When Norbert returned, he took Kit's temperature and gave him more Tylenol. I leaned over and dripped grape juice into his mouth. He slurped it, waved his hand, stared at me. I grabbed his hand and held it tight. He held tight, too.

A man wheeled in the oxygen tank and hooked it up. No smoking near it, he said. When they put the nose piece on Kit, he pulled it off.

"Oxygen! It will help you breathe," I said loudly into his ear.

"NO!" he said.

"Try it!"

He sighed.

"You are the only person he listens to," Rande said gently, and the two of us stood together, our hands on Kit's shoulders and our arms around each other.

In the morning, Robert, Kit's son, and Vincent sat with Kit and I went to Mass at the Epiphany Episcopal Church in downtown Socorro. I saw the priest standing outside the church before the service began, an older man with a warm, jolly face, veins across his cheeks. He saw me coming, and must have seen something more than that because he put out his hands. I took them.

The service was quiet, and the sermon short. In the Episcopal Church the lectionary readings vary year to year in a three-year cycle, but a week after Easter, the Gospel reading is always the same. It's the one about Thomas the Doubter, called the Twin. The other disciples have actually seen Jesus, they tell Thomas. He has appeared to them. He is alive. Thomas says, A man raised from the dead? I have a bridge to sell you. Then Jesus appears to them all again, including Thomas, in a locked room. He stands in front of Thomas and shows him his hands. Thomas steps toward Jesus, and puts his fingers inside the wounds.

Sitting in that pew, I thought of Thomas, a sane person who had never had the experience of seeing someone alive after they had died and may not have wanted to. I understood him. I understood his hesitancy, his wariness, and his desire to see the evidence. He had to feel the wounds. Thomas the Doubter, my twin. But I also understood something else about him. There is a phrase in Spanish: *abrigar esperanzas,* to shelter hope. Thomas may have been working hard not to believe the disciples' story, so to shelter his hope. Hope is like love, maybe worse. It has to do with what is not yet, what is unseen, an architecture of dreams. If Thomas hoped to see Jesus again, and it turned out to be a hoax, what then?

I sat in the pew and cried. No one seemed bothered by it. As I left, the priest offered to come if we needed him.

By afternoon, Kit's breath rattled, his eyes were dark points. "It will be soon," Norbert said.

Vincent and I washed the dinner dishes.

"I am afraid that when he dies, I will die with him," I said.

"Now would be a good time for half a Xanax," Vincent said, handing me a glass to dry.

Kit gurgled when he breathed. I called Norbert to ask if we should move him, help him sit up. No, he said, it's only a matter of hours. Leave him be.

We sat with him in turns, holding his hand. At ten, Rande lay down next to the couch; Vincent and I lay down in her bed. I woke at midnight and lurched into the living room. He was breathing long hollow breaths. At one, I heard Rande talking to him quietly. At 2:30 I woke and rushed into the room.

Everything was still. Nothing moved. The dark night filled the room, filled my heart, filled my brother's lungs. As I waded toward Kit I saw that his hawk nose, his mouth were still in a way they had not been before. It was as if they had settled, sunk. Even as the life in him dwindled, even as I thought when I came into the room earlier and saw him sleeping, Oh, this must be it—no, nothing had been like this. It was as if Kit had gotten up and left his clothes lying on the couch. His hand was cold. The oxygen machine blew useless air. I took the nose piece away from his face, and put my palm against his cheek as I shut off the machine. I brushed his hair back from his forehead, and held my hand against his head.

Then I said, "Rande, Kit has died."

Then it was like a dream. My brother's body white. Norbert arrived at 5:00 a.m. to formally pronounce Kit dead. Rande and I washed him and then wrapped him in a Zuni blanket, placed prayer flags on his chest. Norbert had papers to sign, an inventory of drugs. Rande couldn't fill them out and so I did. Then I stood near the old studio bed in the kitchen, and slowly fainted, the weave of the bedspread on the bed like waves on a lake as I fell. Many people arrived. How did they know? Then the men from Romero's Funeral Home in Belen, in the long white Cadillac hearse with fins, backed up to the garden. Kit's body covered in an orange cloth on the gurney, Robert and Rande and I walked alongside holding on to his feet. The door slammed shut.

INTERLUDE

Rande and I moved through the house, throwing bottles into a garbage bag. We threw away morphine, catheters, laxatives, and Depends and Vicodin and Valium and cans of Ensure. Then I fished out the bottle of Valium and handed it back to her, and we both giggled.

Robert said, "It's April 15. Tax day. At least he died on a day we're all miserable anyway."

We filled two bags, dragged them to the cans outside, past the gourd vine that was flowering yellow bell-shaped flowers; Rita followed behind us, every step.

Get some sleep, Rande said.

I stood in the kitchen holding her hand. Then Vincent and I walked outside and got into the car. I was surprised to be breathing air, to be driving past the junkyard, to see the ruts in the road. My brother was somewhere or maybe he was not. He was here and then he was not. No matter where I went, I would not find him.

At the Holiday Inn, I looked down at the king-sized bed as if it were a swimming pool. I slept as if knocked out. When I woke up, I felt rested and good, then some vague darkness floated into my mind, like that stuff that rises from the bottom of a stagnant pool. Then my brother's death rose up fast, the way a man told me once a shark hit him as he jumped backward off a boat.

I called Mark Asman. At the church, they had trouble finding him. Wait, wait, they said.

When I heard his voice, I started to cry. "So it's done," he said. "I will tell the others. You are in our hearts."

Dickie Romero, who owns Romero's Funeral Home, called me to say he could not cremate my brother because the local doctor, who never saw Kit, would not sign his death certificate. I asked Dickie how long he'd be willing to stay, how late Kit might be cremated, if I got a signature. Dickie said, Go get it. One of Kit's doctors from Albuquerque drove to his office and faxed a signature.

I paced the hotel room, fought with Vincent, then got in the car. I didn't know where I was going, but I headed south and ended up at the Bosque del Apache. When I got out there, the light was turning to evening. I drove out to one of the dikes, and then pulled over and parked. None of the fancy birds were left: the sandhill cranes were gone as well as the snow geese. But there were red-winged blackbirds, Canada geese, and ducks, making their soft sounds. The light was falling evenly on the bull rushes, the yellow millet, and the water. A raven was dive-bombing each pond and the little birds rose and flocked before him and then settled back. Very suddenly, for the first time in months, I felt comforted. Here was life—birds, rushes, and water.

I was looking out at the bull rushes when I saw something else. I saw, or understood, that Kit was there. His singular, unique life. He was there somehow, burning in the rushes, in the light and in the birds. It was as if his life was exploding into them, and was about to become them, and I had been given the miraculous luck to catch him just as he dove in. He was traveling at a great speed, it seemed to me, into the place where all things are alive. I reached toward him, hardly able to believe it, wanting to hold on to him and to the moment, sheltering my hope in doubt. I thought, He is alive.

All of this happened in an instant. I stood out on the dike

next to the car, and watched the water. Then I drove back to the hotel. Dickie Romero had just called. My brother's body had been cremated.

The Hours
of the Cross

❧

1997

1

On January 6, at the Epiphany dinner at church, sixty people had signed up but a hundred attended. A parishioner, Dick Defreitis, asked Anne Howard to bless the salmon because there were only two of them. She blessed them and also the bread. The salmon lasted easily through the evening, and there were baskets of bread left over. "Anne," Dick said, "go easy next time."

We met at Elizabeth's apartment for our January discernment meeting. She lived in a Spanish-style retirement community that sprawled over low hills next to one of our city parks.

Rather than one of her usual suits, Elizabeth wore a pink velour bathrobe and complained of vague stomach distress. We had begun to worry about her. She was after all in her nineties but we had grown so used to her strength and vitality, we were not prepared for any decline. She sat us down at her mahogany dining table, and passed a plate of stale Pepperidge Farm cookies.

All around us were photographs, letters, and books with letters and postcards stuffed inside them—I once opened a book on the Corrigans' shelf and a letter from Daniel Berrigan fell out—a record of eighty years in the church. Signed Sister Corita prints hung on the wall. Next to Elizabeth's elbow was a photo of Dan taken in 1958, when he was fifty-eight, in the chapel at Colorado College. He is just about to rise to his feet to speak. His head is thrown back and his large hands, resting on his knees, are like two nets about to lift him up. We called it, "Dan in Ecstasy."

Elizabeth often spoke as if Dan, who had been dead for three years, were in the next room. "Dan and I," she would say. "Dan and I think." She signed her letters "Elizabeth and Daniel."

Throughout our discernment meetings, she told stories about him, his priesthood, and their life together. I could see that Elizabeth used this time not only to help me discern my direction but to discern how Dan's vocation had affected her life.

This is a story she told us last fall. It was the Depression. Two sons to feed. They were so poor they had been without meat for weeks. At this she looked at me pointedly. I wondered what I was supposed to be hearing. She asked Dan to go up into the church belfry and bag a few baby pigeons, "squab." Dan didn't want to do it, but finally he acquiesced. He came back with two birds that he threw on the table, and then couldn't eat.

"He told me he would never do it again," she said. "He told me the birds trusted the church to live in, just as the people did, and we had broken that trust."

Then she looked at me again.

In Dan's first parish, she told us, his sexton was a beekeeper and a communist.

"He disliked priests, but he liked Dan. He used to come and talk to him about things, the rights of workers and the war in Spain. He would not come to church. I don't think he ever did."

We asked her once what it had been like for her when Dan decided to (illegally) ordain the eleven women in Philadelphia. Elizabeth was quiet and then said, quickly and sharply, "I told him not to do it."

"What was that?" we asked.

"I told him not to ordain them," Elizabeth said. "I told him that we risked being censured and I couldn't live without the church."

"What did he say?" we asked.

"He said he had to do it anyway," Elizabeth replied.

Ann Jaqua said to me later, "She's afraid, you know."

"What of?" I asked.

"She's afraid you're going to be a priest like Dan."

I heard in her stories not only the price she paid for being married to a man who broke rules, but also the sacrifice, the poverty of priesthood. She told us of clothing herself from the church "barrel," the clothing parishioners gave away to the poor. I knew that priesthood in my day was still a financial sacrifice but it was not like that. And Elizabeth knew, how well she knew, the role she had played in Dan's vocation. Once when a young member at Trinity was elected to the vestry, she took his wife aside.

"Congratulations on being elected to the vestry," Elizabeth said.

"Oh, Elizabeth," said Marjorie, worrying that perhaps Elizabeth had had a senior moment. "It was David who was elected."

"I know, dear," said Elizabeth. "I know."

A few weeks before our discernment meeting, Elizabeth had sat next to Vincent at a dinner the monks at Mt. Calvary gave for their friends in the community. She greeted him, sipped from her glass of sherry, nibbled a bit of brie, and then said, "She can't do it without you."

"I'm sorry, Elizabeth," Vincent replied, "I don't understand you."

"She can't be a priest without your support," Elizabeth said. "She can't do it without you."

Because of Kit's death, the discernment committee and I had decided that I should not apply to the diocese for the ministry study year in 1996, but rather wait, continue our deliberations, and apply in 1997. The deadline for the committee's report was coming in May.

That day at Samarkand, we sat in silence and then Ann Jaqua asked, "What have you learned so far from your brother's death and its aftermath that might relate to your discernment?"

I went back to the day right after his death. Vincent and I had driven to Belen, about twenty miles north of Polvadera. The funeral home was a few blocks off the main drag, with a large parking lot and wrought iron bars on the windows. We sat in a small waiting room, with plastic flowers in a tall vase, on an old leather upholstered couch with buttons. Dickie Romero's secretary brought us a square box, a little smaller than a cake box. It was heavy and had a solidity, like that of a newly born baby, as if all of Kit were compressed, packed down. In the car, I carried it on my knees. We took a back road along the river. Willows were leafing out. At Kit's house, Rande was hanging white sheets on a line. She sat down on an old folding aluminum chair with wide strips of striped plastic and took the box into her hands.

"I have a pottery jar," she said. "Let me show you."

Vincent and I decided to spend a few days in Santa Fe while Rande went off to camp at Elephant Butte. On our way out of town, Robert met us and led us to a brass USGS surveyor's cap at Vertical 1, on the low-flow channel of the Rio Grande between the two beautiful towns of San Acacia and Polvadera. On the cap was stamped "KIT." Kit's colleagues had picked up Robert and taken him there the day Kit died and helped him make the name with a jeweler's stamp.

Midweek, Rande called and said Kit's friends had chosen Saturday to gather, and would I lead the service for him.

As I planned the service, I thought about the gathering of people who were his friends, all of whom were so far out of the church that it was not even on their radar screens. I thought of Ben, my friend who died of AIDS and how the prior at the monastery, Robert Hagler, made a ritual of scattering his ashes. How do you make a ritual, I thought. What does it contain? Why do so many of them appear stilted or fall short of fully venerating the human life that has passed? In some ways, I thought, it would be better to simply honor the dead with silence so that we were not misled into believing that words could fill their absence.

I called Donna, Kit's friend, who had known just how to relieve Kit's thirst in his last days by putting juice on a sponge and gently placing it in his mouth. I told her that people would want to wash their hands after scattering the ashes. Will you make a ritual out of it? I asked, not knowing how to explain it and worrying that she would not get it. Yes, she replied.

On Saturday morning, we met at Kit's house. Donna and her teenage daughter arrived with bowls and towels. I thought I'd ask her what she planned, but forgot.

We drove up San Lorenzo Canyon on an old streambed, and stopped at a willow tree fed by a hidden spring. As we gathered, I looked at Kit's friends. They reminded me of something I couldn't quite place. They were big men, hardworking: builders, contractors, surveyors. Many of them drank too much, had lived lives long on the margins; you could see the wounds in their eyes. Part of how they lived was out of choice and part was not. What was clear was that they had given up many things in their lives, but they had not given up their hearts.

I said my eulogy and Vincent read a poem he'd written for Kit. Robert read a poem our parents had sent. Michele read Jane Kenyon's villanelle "Evening," which my cousin Nan had sent to Rande, with its beautiful repeating line, "Let evening come."

Kit's boss stood up and said a few words. He was a big man with a beer belly. Kit picked up how to sight a scope in only a couple of weeks, he said. Another man wearing a beaded jacket did what he called a Native American chant. Kit's former sister-in-law, from the Zuni nation, swung her black hair back.

Rande held Kit's ashes in a bowl. They were not ashes, but bits of bone. We stood in line and scooped them up.

I threw them into the willow, under it, on the sand, at the rock. They blew back at me, stuck to my skirt. I saw the white lying on the mud under the branches. And then I moved toward Donna. She held the wide basin of water in front of her. Next to her was her daughter, holding a stack of clean towels. I centered myself on the bowl. She held it as she had held Kit's head when she was feeding him juice. She met my eyes. I placed my hands on top of the water and let them fall in. When I took them out, she leaned forward with tender mercy and kissed me gently on the mouth. And it came to me who Kit's friends reminded me of as my tears fell into the bowl, these people on the borders of respectability, "outside the church"—this was what the disciples must have been like.

In the late afternoon, Vincent and I sat on the couch where Kit had died. I drank wine straight from a bottle at my feet. My experience at the Bosque seemed far away, and because it was so strange, and I had very little to compare it to, I couldn't call it back without doubting that I'd had it. And, it seemed too singular, too unrelated. What was its use? I thought. What was the point of seeing, briefly, that someone was alive, somewhere? Now, where he had been there was a hole. As we live, my friend Jodie says, we carry around more and more holes left by the people we have loved. Older and older, more and more of them. Rande traveled around and through the house and the garden. Rita followed her, ears flopped down. Then the time came. We kissed Rande good-bye in the yard. "I can't see you drive away," she said. I held on to the car seat and the door as we drove. When we got to the airport, I said, "I can't get on the plane," and Vincent said, "Yes, you can."

Ann Jaqua said quietly, "I hope you realize that you were their priest that day."

Then I told them, in whatever words I could find, about the time at the Bosque del Apache.

Mark Benson listened, his face still as a rock.

"When Phil died, the one question I had was, where is he? I still go back to the moment when he stopped breathing and I feel the goosebumps roll over me as he enters the Other Realm. And there was this huge question there, hanging, hanging. I asked a priest, 'Where is Phil?' And he gave me some hackneyed Christian line about where the dead go. I think he quoted some piece of scripture. It meant nothing to me.

"When Phil comes to me in my dreams and I see him usually now alive and well, I still ask in my mind, 'Well, Philip, where are you? Where did you go?'

"You know," he said, looking at me, "a priest ought to be able to answer those questions."

Mark called me later and said, "While I was hiking up Tunnel Trail, I was thinking about what we talked about and I realized that I needed back then for the priest to enter into poetry, because that is where Phil is. He could have said, 'Well, Phil is at the zoo now.' Something that would clearly express the fact that he is gone, no longer literal, not here, not visible, but not absent, not without influence, not dead. The problem with the priest's response was that it was literal, and Phil is not literal anymore! That's why poetry and art are so important, because that's where he is.

"And to go on preaching my little sermonette here, that's what ails Christianity, this literalness, this imprisonment with the facts of history. When it becomes this, with the insistence on historical authenticity and whether the water really became wine and Jesus literally being raised from the dead, then it loses its whole point, which is to show me where Phil is and to show us how to relate to the earth and be comfortable with mystery. I needed the response to transport me to Phil, to just send me there to the spirit world. If only the priest had just quoted some T. S. Eliot! Like "Little Gidding"! That would have done it."

As I listened to Mark, I thought how the discernment of "my" call might be a larger working out of things left undone in each of our lives. It was like diving together into a realm of otherness, below the waves, and rising with treasure to the surface. We were speaking of things "not literal" and they had, like the pottery jars found in the granaries at Chaco Canyon, a fragility born of being left untended in dim and shadowed light. They needed to be spoken of in a place that was like an intermediate room between two worlds, a place that wouldn't break them, nor expose them too soon to the harsh air.

2

The vestry took a weekend in February to talk business at Mt. Calvary Monastery. I drove up with George Barrett, the retired bishop. The road to the monastery wound up into Santa Barbara's foothills, past an old mission irrigation system, and a new city reservoir, and up onto a more treacherous road with sharp curves and precipitous drops. George, eighty-eight, was driving.

He drove with both hands on the lower third of the steering wheel, peering through thick glasses at the top of the wheel, finding his way, his grandson said once, "by divination."

"Good driving, George," I said hoping that encouragement would improve his skills.

"Great going!" I yelled as he swerved to miss an SUV barreling down the hill towards us.

George muttered, "We're not there yet."

At the monastery parking area, George and I unpacked the car.

As we walked toward the front portal, I turned to gaze at the hills above us and then down at the ocean in the distance, a misty blue horizon, the islands drifting in the fog. One of the monks had placed new gravel, called Palm Springs Gold, near the front porch. The thick oak door opened with a smooth rush of air, and we were greeted by the now-familiar view of a salon of polished red oak floors sweeping a hundred feet toward a gold Spanish altar at the far end. Thick oriental rugs were spread in rich splendor on the floors. A bowl of freshly picked pink camellias lay upon a heavy antique table. Brother Roy's calligraphy ("The

Glory of God is the Human Person Fully Alive"), Brother Nick's watercolors, and old oil paintings graced the walls. Through huge glass doors midway down the room, lawns, gardens, wrought iron tables, and chairs beckoned. To our noses wafted the scent of roasting meat.

"If this is poverty," said a Franciscan monk on opening the door, "I'd like to see chastity."

I was rooming with Terry Roof, a member of the vestry, in the "bishops' room," a large bedroom with portraits of various misanthropic bishops on the walls in ruffled shirts and two high twin beds in separate alcoves. We chose it because it had a bathtub. Our plan was to combine vestry business with our own spa weekend. I brought a large jar of green facial clay from France.

Outside in the courtyard garden, bees lingered over blue rosemary blossoms and lizards did push-ups in the waning sun. Then the monks said vespers and we settled into a sumptuous dinner of roast pork and homemade applesauce. Before I left the house, Vincent, who had been cleaning out our cupboards, handed me a bottle of barbeque sauce. "We'll never use this," he said, "Tell the monks I donate it to them."

I handed the jar of sauce to Timothy Jolley, a tall, round monk with red-blond hair. Timothy came to the Order in 1973 after a teaching career at the University of North Carolina. He said once in a sermon that the psychiatrist who interviewed him before he entered the Order asked him why he was choosing this life.

"Why are you joining the Order?"

"Because I feel that God is calling me to this life," Timothy replied.

"Whether it was God or your own fantasy," the psychiatrist replied, "you are here, so let's talk about that."

Timothy took the jar, weighed it in his palm, and grinned.

"Thank Vincent for the donation," he said, "but do tell him: this is so heavy and a check is so light."

The vestry gathered in the monastery's largest meeting room around a large fireplace, well stocked with oak logs. Tonight, as a way to connect to each other and help the three new vestry members become acclimatized, we filled out forms to determine our place on what is called the enneagram scale. Most of the vestry turned out to be middle-of-the-roaders, balanced, observing "sixes." But a newly elected lawyer and I were "ones," in the wisdom of the enneagram: "perfectionist reformers." Mark glanced at us over his glasses and sighed.

We said compline with the monks that evening, at 8:00 p.m., and slowly began to enter into their rhythm of prayer. At the end of the service, Robert sang, in a light voice, "Guardian angels God will send thee, all through the night," and we were sent off to sleep.

In the morning, we prayed with the monks at 7:30, then ate a quick, silent breakfast, and gathered in the south library, a sunny room with a smaller fireplace trimmed in polished wood, bookcases on four walls (novels, biographies, and histories), and a wide window facing the ocean. Anne Howard and Martha Seigel, another priest who works at Trinity, met with us briefly to talk about inclusive language in liturgy. They asked each of us to draw what God looked like, with crayons on large pieces of artist's paper. I don't think anyone drew an old man sitting on a throne in heaven. Mainly we tried to draw light, or some approximation of light, and color.

We planned to spend the morning focused on same-sex blessings, and there was a feeling of tension and excitement in the air. Mark said a prayer, and made a few opening remarks. He summarized how we had arrived at this point, and reminded us that the human sexuality committee had studied the issue thoroughly and was asking us to act.

Marriage had a social and legal function, he pointed out, and was not part of the church, not a sacramental rite of the church, until the Middle Ages. There were monogamous and polygamous marriages in legal history, but monogamy was the most common. Then he talked about blessings, and the need for homosexual couples to have their unions blessed by the church.

George Barrett cleared his throat and said that the purpose of marriage historically was for procreation, for children, for the ordering of sex, and for companionship.

"I see no reason why the rector of Trinity can't preside at the blessing of a same-sex union. I think that the congregation is ready for it."

"What is likely to be the reaction from the larger church?" Terry Roof asked.

"That depends on who or what you mean by the larger church," George replied. "I think if we are quiet about it, if we don't make it into a media circus, nothing much will be said at the diocesan level."

"Do you think we should call them blessings or marriage?" I asked.

"I think blessings," George replied. "I don't think people are ready to call a ceremony between two persons of the same sex 'marriage.' "

"But the argument that makes the most sense to me," someone else said, "is that we don't want to withhold a sacrament of the church from anyone, be they gay or straight, and that sacrament is marriage."

"It's actually a sacramental rite," George said. "The only sacraments in the church are baptism and the Eucharist. But in any case, while that may be true, I think we are talking about what is possible in our current political environment. It may be a compromise, to call them blessings rather than marriage, but I think that is where we are, right now."

There was a little pause in the conversation, and then Colleen Sterne, a lawyer, new to the vestry, who had been silent, spoke up.

"I've been thinking about marriage," she said. "Marriage is

the single, central fact of my existence. My husband and I have a diverse set of friends who are either gay or lesbian or straight or undecided, and I am struck by how 'blessings' sounds to me like the same language used to justify racial discrimination. 'Separate but equal' is the phrase that comes to mind. Marriage is everything to me, I have derived strength from my monogamous marriage, it's changed and deepened over the nearly twenty years we've been together, and I've gone places I never thought I or my marriage would go. How can we say that we're going to deprive people of this, because they are gay? Aren't we saying to them your relationships are good, but they are not quite good enough?"

Colleen continued, "One of the gifts of a long-term monogamous relationship, especially one strengthened with marriage vows, is its fruitfulness, its ability to constitute more than a sum of its parts. For some this may mean children, but for others it can mean different things. A good marriage produces a generative force, a creative impulse, that works to the benefit of both partners, and produces good things at every level of community, from family and friends to the world. Jim and I don't have children, but I feel that our relationship has been downright prolific! We play a role in the lives of young people, from our nieces, nephews, and godchildren to unrelated children in the community. It is the same for many couples without children that I know. We need all kinds of families—some to raise children, some to focus on the raising up of all children, and some to raise up other things for the good of the community."

When Colleen had finished speaking, silence filled the room, and I thought, Draw that silence, and you will have drawn God.

"The idea that marriage should be somehow watered down, that there's something that precludes gay people from being able to enter it, seems entirely wrong to me," Colleen continued. "It seems entirely wrong."

George rested his chin on his hand.

"I understand what you are saying," he said and then was quiet.

"That is such a beautiful description of marriage," I said. "And I think once you get into the blessing arena, it becomes muddy. The argument that makes the most sense to me is that marriage, as a sacrament or sacramental rite of the church, should not be withheld from someone because he or she is gay. That no sacrament should be withheld from anyone on the basis of sexuality."

Bob, a member of the vestry who was gay, said he wasn't sure he wanted the "commitment ritual" for homosexual couples to be called marriage.

"I have trouble with the baggage associated with the word," he said. "And I know a lot of other gay guys do, too. I think the human sexuality committee wanted us to approve blessings, not marriage."

Mark said crossly, "That is not really up to the human sexuality committee. This is a vestry decision."

Mark tapped his hand on his knee. "I was thinking," he said later. "Is marriage possible for gay men? Would it be welcome? Could I or other gay men uphold those beautiful and solemn vows?"

We were training ourselves to walk out on a limb, I thought, feeling for our feet along the branch as it narrowed and swayed.

Finally George spoke quietly, as if only to Colleen. "You have convinced me," he said.

"Somehow I don't feel as if there should be a vote on this," Mark said, "although I want to make sure we have all agreed. Are we agreed?"

No one spoke. I looked over at Bob. He was looking at his hands.

The next orders of business fell into line: Colleen would head a committee that would review the guidelines for holy matrimony that Trinity gives prospective couples seeking to be married in the church. She would comb it for language that excluded gay or lesbian couples, and suggest changes and additions.

"With the rector's approval," George said.

"With the rector's approval," Colleen said and smiled.

"Such as how to deal with couples who can't be legally married, according to state law, which is, of course, a problem for gays and lesbians," Mark added.

"How shall we announce this to the congregation?" I asked.

"Should we send a letter?" someone said. "Or just announce it in the newsletter?"

"I think a newsletter article is sufficient," Mark replied.

"I don't," Terry said. "I think we need a letter."

"I think people are weary of the subject, frankly," someone said. "I think another letter is overkill."

"But this is a big step," I said, uncertain.

We talked over exactly how to announce our decision and the majority felt that a simple newsletter announcement, followed by a parish-wide evening meeting to discuss how the vestry arrived at the decision, was all that was necessary. Colleen would write the newsletter article. I felt uneasy. The word "marriage" had never been used in the context of homosexual relationships at Trinity.

At five minutes to noon, one of the monks rang a bell in the courtyard, calling us to the Eucharist in the chapel. When we straggled in, most of the monks were already seated in the pews in their hooded white habits, under which Birkenstocks and running shoes peeked out. When we exchanged the peace half way through the service, this step we had taken together moved through us, connecting and revitalizing us. It was as if we were beads on a string. As I wished George and then Colleen "Peace be with you," I thought about how this peace of God was not a comfortable heaven where everyone was nice to each other but a baptism of movement and action, creating a different kind of peace in its wake. One of the younger monks, Robert Sevensky, preached a sermon that he began and ended with a Buddhist evening *gatha:*

"Awake! Awake! Awake! Do not squander your life."

The monks served dinner after the Eucharist. George Barrett sat down to his plate of roast chicken and garlic-soaked spinach. I sat next to him.

"What do you think of all this, George?" I asked.

He growled, then held up his hand. He removed his hearing aid, picked up a nearby butter knife, and began making small adjustments to a screw.

"Say it again," he said, returning the aid to his ear.

I did, and he replied, "I am convinced this is the right course to take in the interests of justice," and returned to the chicken.

In the early evening, we said vespers with the monks, praying a selection of psalms in quavering sing-song. The services were like bookends for the day. In the chapel, the air felt sweetened, almost oxygenated. I looked out the window toward the hills below the chapel and saw that the light was falling on an oak tree in a slightly different way than it had the evening before. What would it be like to watch that tree at the same time every day, day after day, year after year? What would I see? It struck me that, apart from simple discipline, we are asked to pray at the same hour every day so that we may be witnesses to the world, to its changing beauty.

As the weekend wore on, we slowly wound down, spending much of Sunday on more conventional vestry business: electing a junior warden, appointing council chairs. At the end, Mark, in a V-neck sweater and khakis, dark circles under his eyes, was cleaning up the library when another visitor to the monastery, a friendly man who loves to hug, moved toward him, a gleam in his eye.

"No," Mark shouted at him. "Please not now!"

"Long weekend?" I muttered.

"Long weekend," he sighed.

When I opened the door at home, no one greeted me. I finally found Vincent outside in the garden, smoking. "Oh," he said, "hi. I didn't know you had come home. Weren't you supposed to come home earlier?" I sat down with him and stammered an apology about being late. The truth was that I had hung out with Mark in the afternoon at the monastery after the other vestry members had left, talking over the decision we had made, gossiping, debriefing. I had not thought about Vincent at home, waiting.

"This is how it's going to be," he said, with a nasty and uncertain smile. "Just like this. Long weekends, late coming home. I'm going to hate the priesthood."

"Oh, great, thanks," I said. "Thanks for all the support," and walked back into the house, slamming the French-paned door. The irony of my situation was not lost on me. I had spent the weekend defending marriage and the beauty of the marriage vows, and acting to extend its grace to those deprived of it while all the while my own marriage was falling into slammed doors and sniping.

It took the vestry a month to figure out the wording of the newsletter article, and in April's newsletter, it finally appeared, right along with prayers for those about to be confirmed in the church and an announcement of a spring tea, under the headline, "April 22 Panel Discussion on Same-Sex Unions."

"At the vestry retreat in February, we spent a morning with Bishop George Barrett and Mark Asman discussing same-sex covenants, marriage, and guidelines for couples (both heterosexual and homosexual) who wish to marry," Colleen had written. "As a result of that discussion, we came to the position that we are going to use the same language to characterize the unions of both homosexual couples and heterosexual couples. Both will be called marriage." The article invited the parish to a panel discussion with vestry members on April 22.

"Hold on to your garter belts," I said to Mark.

"It will be fine," he said.

A few days before April 15, my body knew before my mind could comprehend that the one-year anniversary of Kit's death was coming up. I ached; I hurt all over. Then my thoughts shifted back toward New Mexico, and the last gray days of his life. Rande sent me one of his shirts, purple and red flannel squares, and I wore it in the early mornings, rubbing my hands along its sleeves. I asked her how she was doing and she replied, "I am actually doing well," and then told me she planned to marry again, one of Kit's friends, also a surveyor. I was glad for her, I said, and I was. But when I hung up I felt a deep fury that someone else would be living in my brother's house with Rande, and a deep cold regret that I had not been ordained in time to officiate at Kit and Rande's wedding, which now would never be.

The phone rang and it was Kit's son, Robert. "I went out to Kit's surveyor's cap," he said. "And I polished it with some brass polish."

"I wish I'd been with you," I said.

"Me, too," he said.

I sat down after talking to Robert and thought where Kit might be, now, where his living breath had gone. And I thought about my life since Kit had died. Kit's death itself had released me from old obligations for a while, so I had more time, and the urgency and despair I felt had forced me to pray or form words that might be prayers. The meetings with the discernment committee had taught me to honor listening. I was closer to Robert, a nephew I had always loved but never known as an adult. I had grown more used to questions that might not, at that moment, have an answer. I could see that something had been given to me, but I could not put a name to it, not yet.

But I didn't consciously register the long-haul cost of going through my brother's death, and then launching into a discernment process (while holding down a job, writing, and being married). I didn't notice how tired or how irritable I was or how little I was giving to Vincent.

On April 22, the evening was chilly, but sweet-smelling, as night-blooming jasmine filled the air. In the guild hall a table and five chairs were set up facing rows of Trinity's ubiquitous white, uncomfortable, folding chairs. As I entered the room, I noticed a frail man with wispy brown hair sitting off near the fireplace, and finally I placed him. He was from a conservative Episcopal church in town. We'd served food together at the soup kitchen and got along despite our different theological and political beliefs. His church was against the ordination of gay priests, inclusive language, and certainly, oh, certainly, same-sex marriage. Why was he here, I thought. How did he hear about it?

Colleen, Mark, and several other vestry members seated themselves at the table. By this time, the room was full. The atmosphere did not feel comfortable; it felt somewhere between tense and expectant.

Colleen summarized the decision-making of the vestry, but did not repeat the moving description of marriage she had given at the vestry retreat. George and Mark made brief speeches about marriage and the church, and they opened the floor to questions.

Several older women raised their hands. One by one they said they supported the relationships of gay people but that they objected to the vestry's decision to call same-sex blessings "marriage." It became clear that they saw it as a betrayal: marriage had never been mentioned in all of our congregation-wide discussions. In all the work we had done to make this pathway smooth, we had fallen down here, and now they were as upset as I had ever seen members of the parish.

"How did the vestry suddenly make this decision?" asked one.

"Marriage is for a man and a woman," said another. "I can't change the way I feel about that."

A wave of distrust was rising. Mark and Colleen looked at each other, then away.

Martha Smith, an elderly woman with neat white hair who ironed linens for the altar guild, rose carefully and said, "I'm sorry, I was married for forty years, and I think marriage is a relationship between a man and a woman."

A young girl raised her hand. "I am a lesbian," she said, "and when I read of this decision it was the first time I felt accepted in a church community." She was crying.

Then the man from the conservative church raised his hand. I looked right at him. He looked down at the floor. He said he was here to "represent" the larger church community, and that they were shocked that we would consider "defaming" marriage this way.

That brought Ann Jaqua to her feet. "Bill, we worked together in the soup kitchen," she said. "We have things we agree on. But I can't hear you say that without speaking out. There are people I love in this room, whom you are insulting. You are insulting gay people by imagining that, if they choose to marry, it would defame the institution."

Bill shook his head. "I can't change the way I feel, the way we feel," he said.

Fred, a gay man, stood in the back of the room. He was a

friend of Bob, the vestry member who had seemed unhappy with our decision.

"I don't know what I think," Fred said. "But I know that I don't like the way this decision was made. In secret."

"It was not made in secret," Colleen snapped.

Finally, Barbara Fazio, a volunteer in the office, stood up shakily, and said, through tears, "I love you, Mark, but I don't agree with this decision."

"Well, I love you, too, Barbara," Mark said softly. "And I hope this community can be a place where we can talk."

Finally nearly everyone left, in different states, many of them unknown and probably unfathomable to me. Nothing was settled. I was walking into the kitchen when I overheard a conversation taking place inside and stopped at the door. A professor of history at the university was picking up a couple of dishes left from some potluck past. Carol Lansing, also a professor, of Italian medieval studies, was washing something in the sink. He said to her that he did not understand why we were making such a big deal of all this, that it was "time to move onto other things, and stop talking about homosexuals."

"That's fine for you," Carol said. "But what about them?"

3

Within a few days, the vestry met to discuss what had happened on April 22. We quickly divided into two camps: One wanted to write a letter to the parish and have another parish-wide forum to explain our process in greater detail, educate people further about marriage and same-gender couples, and apologize for the way the "marriage issue" was handled. A second group had had enough of meetings and letters, and simply wanted to go forward. I was in the first camp. We finally agreed to go ahead with a letter and a forum.

"Is there any sense that we should revisit our decision about marriage?" Mark asked.

No one spoke, then Colleen said, "No, it was and is the right thing."

"I think the decision was right," Mark Asman said. "But the process as to how we moved from 'blessing' to 'marriage' was certainly less than perfect."

Three of us volunteered to write the letter: Leslie, a woman who works as an admissions director at the university; Bob, the gay man who didn't like the idea of using the term "marriage"; and me. "Be positive," Mark's notes read. "Be empathic. Bring closure. Bring closure to the process."

Over the weekend, however, I had a change of heart. I called Stephen Gibson and said, "I don't think we should have another forum after all. Just a letter. And I'm not sure about the apology. We have some explaining to do, but we're not really in the wrong."

"I've been thinking the same thing," he replied. We decided to call Mark, and the other vestry members, to poll them on our new thoughts. Everyone agreed that we should drop the forum idea; two thought we should drop the letter. I called them both and promised to take their concerns to the meeting of the letter-writing committee, thinking to myself, one more meeting and I will drop the letter idea myself.

We met, and began a draft letter, starting with history: "Two years ago, Trinity began a journey as a community to explore the complexity of human sexuality."

Leslie agreed to draft our ideas further, and send them around by email. But within twenty-four hours, I received an email from Bob complaining about the decision to drop the forum. "I am having a hard time with your 180-degree change on the follow-up forum," he wrote. I tried to explain my change of heart, and received an email that read, "I am disturbed by the tactics you, Steve (and Mark?) used to sway the vestry...." Then Fred, Bob's friend, sent me an email that read, in part, "The trust level [in the parish] is everlastingly damaged."

As I looked up from my computer I thought about something George Barrett had said to me, early in the discernment process: "Very little time in a priest's life is spent on 'holy' things. Most of it is conflict management and resolution."

Or, as a woman priest said in a sermon on ordination, "There are times when the church is like a swimming pool: all the noise comes from the shallow end."

Within days, Bob resigned from the vestry.

The letter, in its final form, reiterated the vestry decision step by step. In part it read,

> Christian marriage is a covenant between two people. Its intention is to be lifelong; it is monogamous and procreative or generative. It provides a place for healthy sexual relationships and companionship. Even if children

are not born of a marriage, it creates a new life in the world. It unites two lives so they become, in a mysterious way, a third life that supports friends, family and contributes to the stability of the larger community. With this understanding, we realized we did not wish to institute a "separate but equal service" for gay and lesbian persons, a service that might actually diminish the profound nature of marriage. We also decided that the same standards of commitment, responsibility, and relationship to the community of faith must equally apply to both heterosexual and homosexual relationships. In essence, the rector and vestry believe that the Church cannot offer another sacrament for the blessing of the union of two persons other than marriage and that the sacramental rite of marriage must be open to all people.

The day the letter was mailed, Mark called me. "Two members of the parish, two men, have asked me to officiate at their wedding," he said. "Charles and Philip."

"When is their date?" I asked.

"September 28th," he replied.

There were only a few reactions to the letter. The professor of history who had talked in the kitchen about his views on homosexuals resigned from the parish. A couple wrote a note thanking the vestry for explaining their decision in such detail; it would help them explain it to their child. A few people made appointments with Mark to express their ongoing concern, but they did not leave the parish. It felt as if people were waiting, but for what?

.   .   .

In this atmosphere, Charles and Philip sent out their wedding invitations.

I was enjoying so much work in the church, running off to meetings in the evenings and then cramming in as much as my day job would allow. Vincent seemed more and more grumpy and less and less available as the spring wore on.

I don't know how the fight began, or how it got to the point where I opened the door of a moving car. Vincent was shouting, "Fuck you, fuck you, fuck you." And I was screaming, "Stop. Stop. Stop this fucking car." Then I opened the door, and took a look at a moving sidewalk. He stopped. I got out. He drove away.

On the counselor's bookshelf was the title *Pathos and Eros*. I stared at the book and thought, How apt, as I listened to Vincent talk. I stared at her bookcase because I couldn't look at his face.

The therapist, who happened to be a Roman Catholic by upbringing, asked him what image he had of a priest.

"A person who is on call twenty-four hours a day," he replied. "A person who has meetings in the evenings, and on the weekends, who is rarely available. Who has given her life to a parish. And to something I don't believe in: God and the church, or the church's God."

That about nails it, I thought.

"The problem," he said turning to me, "is that I think you'd make a very good parish priest." His voice shook. "I just don't want you to do it."

I looked down at my hands and cried. It was the first time he'd said that he thought I'd make a good priest. I can't choose between Vincent and the church, I thought. I don't believe that any God that I love would ask me to.

"There's something else," Vincent said later. "I know that you being a priest is not something I want for me but I don't know if this is something I want for you. When you used to come home from the soup kitchen, you were lighter. You weren't trying to control it. Now when you come home from church meetings, you are full of planning and intrigue. It sounds like a job. Only there is no product.

"Do you remember when Elizabeth said to me that you couldn't do it without me?"

"Yes," I said.

"I didn't really know what to say to her," he said. "I knew that it was so. But I wanted to say, 'It's not what I wish for her.' "

The next day, I met with the discernment committee. After about twenty minutes of silence, Mark Benson said, "I wonder if the question is changing. I knew it would change. Is the question changing for you, Nora?"

I looked down at the table.

"It feels as if the question was, Does Nora have a vocation? But now it's different," Mark said. "Now it is not, Does she have a vocation, but. . . ." He stopped.

Ann said, "How does it play out."

"Exactly," Mark said.

I felt at once released and imprisoned.

Ann said, "I felt called once, years ago, not to priesthood, but to a new life; it was so intense. I woke up in the night. I felt as if everything counted, nothing could be left out."

"Yes," I said, feeling a wave of relief. "Nothing can be left out."

Then I turned to them and asked, "Is something happening to you?"

Mark nodded.

I said, "I wonder what that is about. I mean, I think you're not going to get off scot-free."

They laughed. Ann said, "You'll notice she says that with delight."

Mark said, "Maybe we will discern everyone's vocation."

When I told Mark Asman about that session he said, "Hold that in the palm of your hand."

4

In 1968, Sue Hiatt, a social worker in New Haven, drew a chart called a "force field analysis," which was taught to her when she was in graduate school. She took a sheet of paper and wrote at the top, "What are the forces that are opposed to one another in the question of women's ordination?" Then she drew a line from top to bottom down the middle of the page. On one side of the line, Sue wrote, "Bishops." Then she drew an arrow pointing toward the line. On the other side of the line, she wrote, "Women who are called." And drew an arrow opposing the first one.

Under bishops, she wrote, "Institutional role. (Only a bishop can ordain a priest.)" Also, "Money." And "PR."

Under women, she wrote, "Called by God."

She surveyed the chart. It did not, she said later, look good. She asked herself, Where can we find money? How can we erode the power base of the House of Bishops? What can we do about PR?

Her first move was to work with friends in seminaries around the country on a series of workshops advertised to women in the church on various theological subjects. At each workshop, held on seminary grounds, women were invited to participate in various discussions, including "Women Who Are Called to Ordination." By collecting the names of women who participated in this workshop, Sue formed a network and she began writing letters. What foundations might support such a movement in the church, she asked. Whom do you know?

Within a few months, she had a grant from a religious foundation to study the role of women's ordination in the church. With this money, she set up an office, printed booklets telling the story of the women who felt they were called, bought stamps, and set up a telephone line.

Under institutional role, she wrote, "Do all bishops feel the same?" and asked her network to suggest the names of bishops who might be persuaded to vote for the ordination of women if it came before the House at general convention.

A few years later, Robert DeWitt, a bishop who had recently resigned from his post, was contemplating an interesting phenomenon. "The women who were graduating from seminary and being ordained as deacons," he recalled, "were more interesting, and smarter, I have to say, than the men. I asked myself, Why is this? And then I said to myself, I wonder if these women should be ordained to the priesthood?"

In a few days, he talked to Sue Hiatt.

In 1974, on July 29, the feast day of Saints Mary and Martha, Bishops DeWitt, Corrigan, and Edward Welles met Sue Hiatt, Carter Heyward, and nine other women in the sacristy of the Church of the Advocate in Philadelphia in the heat and humidity of summer at ten in the morning. Two thousand people waited for them in the sanctuary.

About ten days earlier, the three bishops had written a letter to the wider church: "We intend to ordain to the sacred priesthood some several women deacons," the letter began. The bishops pointed out that they were aware of the "diversity of thinking" in the church on the issue, that there were theological considerations, biblical considerations, and considerations of church tradition. They talked about how the House of Bishops was on record in favor of ordination for women, and that a majority of the House of Deputies were also on record in favor, but that a rule of procedure had frustrated the will of the majority.

Yet "all of these foregoing factors, by themselves, would not necessarily dictate the action we intend," they wrote.

> There is a ruling factor which does require this action on our part. It is our obedience to the Lordship of Christ. . . . Ours is a risen Lord. He was raised in the power of the Spirit so that we might participate, however inadequately, in His triumph over sin and separation, proclaim the good news of His victory, and occasionally ourselves walk in newness of life. . . .
>
> This action is therefore intended as an act of obedience to the Spirit. By the same token, it is intended as an act of solidarity with those in whatever institution, in whatever part of the world, of whatever stratum of society, who, in their search for freedom, for liberation, for dignity, are moved by that same Spirit to struggle against sin, to proclaim that victory, to attempt to walk in newness of life.

At a little after eleven that morning, the bishops laid hands on the heads of the women and they were ordained priests.

Right after the irregular ordinations in Philadelphia, the Presiding Bishop called together in New York a meeting of the bishops who were most opposed to the ordination of women in the hopes of reaching an agreement. Bishop Noland of Louisiana was killed in a plane crash at Kennedy Airport as he flew to the meeting. A few weeks later, all eleven women and the bishops who had ordained them received a letter from Bishop Wolf of Maine, suggesting that the bishop of Louisiana would be alive if they had not done what they had. To which Emily Hewitt, one of the ordinands, responded by sending back a Xerox of the letter along with a brief note: "Dear Bishop Wolf, I should warn you that some yo-yo has gotten hold of your letterhead (see enclosed)."

In July of 1975 George Barrett, now retired and living in Santa Barbara, got a call from Bob DeWitt, telling him of four women who wished to be ordained in Washington, D.C. George said that his personal situation, having been divorced and remarried, might make it inappropriate for him to do this unusual thing.

"Isn't that pretty bad theology?" Bishop DeWitt asked.

"I had to grant that it was," George remembered.

On September 7, 1975, at four o'clock in the afternoon at the church of St. Stephen and the Incarnation in Washington, D.C., Bishop Barrett ordained four more women to the priesthood, also without church permission. (Earlier in the afternoon, a bomb threat caused the police to close the church and bring in dogs to sniff for explosives.) In a letter George wrote to the larger church announcing that he intended to ordain the women, he wrote, "At considerable risk, energy and pain, [the women who wish to be ordained] are leading all of us toward overcoming the sexism which, no less than racism, is a work of death in our time." The bishop of the Diocese of Los Angeles immediately revoked Bishop Barrett's license to preach, ordain, and celebrate the Eucharist for one year.

On September 16, 1976, both the House of Bishops and the House of Deputies voted to amend the canons of the church to provide that women as well as men were eligible for ordination as bishops, priests, and deacons. As of 2002, there are 3,481 women priests in the United States (about 20 percent of all clergy) and ten women bishops.

Shortly after she was ordained a deacon, Carter Heyward was administering the chalice during communion, and was scratched on the hand by a priest (at least he was a man wearing a clerical collar) who told her to "burn in hell."

Fourteen years later, when Anne Howard was newly ordained,

a little boy in her Sunday school classroom drew a picture of God. God had a long flowing robe, and nice gold hoop earrings.

The discernment committee met at Ann Jaqua's house one final time.

"Prophetic," said Ed out of the silence. "What is the difference between a prophet and a priest?"

"Good question," Ann replied. "I think a prophet is someone who inhabits the margins of a society, almost alone."

"What would a prophetic priesthood look like?" Mark Benson asked.

"I guess a prophetic priest would be someone who calls out of the people their gifts and calls the church itself into its future," Ann replied. "Basil Meeking, the Roman Catholic bishop who preached at Dan Corrigan's funeral, said Dan was a man who never lost hope for the future, that he was set free by hope."

"A leadership that is too conservative and rigid is suffocating," said Mark Benson. "And one that is too far out on the margins is too exotic and solitary. A prophetic priesthood exists between these two extremes; it would be generative and procreative."

In their final report, they wrote, "In Nora's work at Trinity we see a prophetic priesthood emerging."

I went home and held that in the palm of my hand. I thought about those women ordained in the seventies. Carter Heyward and Sue Hiatt were teaching at the Episcopal Divinity School in Cambridge, Massachusetts; Lee McGee had recently retired from Yale. One of the Philadelphia Eleven had left the church. I had met Carter, Lee, and Sue. Carter was small and Southern, genteel and rakish. Lee was almost blind; she suffered from a congenital disease of the retina, and when I met her she was training herself to get along with a guide dog, a German Shepherd named Alex. She was teaching women in small groups how to "reclaim their voices," a project she had started with women divinity students who had trouble preaching. Sue was tall and watchful, with a big wide step and hunched shoulders. When she spoke at a dinner here in Santa Barbara, the whole room turned toward her and listened. Each one of them, I realized, was unafraid to exercise what Lee called "agency." Each one was her own authority.

They had each felt some stirring, some ache, toward a vocation that in nearly two thousand years had not seen a woman in its ranks.

Or maybe it had. In its first two hundred years of life, Christianity was practiced in house churches. Because women often administered households (including overseeing large staffs of servants and slaves), they became leaders in those churches. Karen Torjesen, in her book *When Women Were Priests,* said that house churches and the leadership of women made the early church "informal, often countercultural in tone, and marked by a fluidity and flexibility. . . ."

They could have been places where, for a few short hours, servant and master, men and women, slaves and free, and (I will bet you) gay and straight became equals. In short, a company of friends.

"And this is what we mean by friends," said Cicero. "Even when they are absent, they are with us; even when they lack some things, they have an abundance of others; even when they are weak, they are strong; and, harder still, even when they are dead, they are alive."

I began the fourteen-question diocesan application. I didn't feel like an emerging prophetic priest. I felt like a cross between a college applicant and a lottery hopeful. I answered question eight, "Turning points in your life" and number nine, "Your understanding of the differences between a priest and a deacon."

I answered the supplemental question "Marriage" with restrained anxiety. Vincent had to write a page on his view of marriage as well. (Too many persons had actually entered the process without telling their spouses.) Vincent tapped on the door of my study and handed me a sheet of paper. At the top was written: "Husband's statement."

"My idea of marriage is that it is the intimate union of two people; that this union creates a common life that has a life and strength (and burdens) of its own. I like the image, in Ecclesiastes, of the three-fold cord not quickly broken." I smiled at the biblical reference. I knew he'd searched for a metaphor that could be read by those who spoke "religion."

"Although I am tone deaf to the promptings of religion I've come to the point where I am happy to see Nora come into her own in a part of her life that's important to her, proud of her too. . . ." Here, I began to cry.

"Seminary and ordination will bring further change. I can't predict what shape that change will take, except that it will be. During those years, to stay together, we will need to attend to our common life closely rather than let it go dry or too hungry; we can't presume that it will somehow survive on its own or that we can always rescue it later. Knowing this as a kind of basic ground, a lesson learned, is all I can know, going in." I put the sheet of paper down on my lap and thought, All this time I've been so caught up in the church and the struggle of discernment, and he's been sitting in the next room, thinking.

Mark sat down and wrote his letter of recommendation. In the letter to him sent by the diocese, they thanked him for his work, and remarked, "It will be helpful in discerning a vacation."

"I wouldn't mind discerning a vacation," Mark remarked.

Ann Jaqua typed the discernment committee's final report. I sent out four requests for letters of reference (two clergy, two lay). My college sent a transcript. My math teacher at St. John's sent a letter explaining a poor grade in analytic geometry. A medical report, including a complete physical (the mental stuff would come later that year in the form of the dreaded Minnesota Multiphasic), an occupational history, a letter from my spiritual director, and five passport-sized photos. I drove down to the local police station and had my fingerprints taken in a dim hallway by a policeman who hardly spoke. At the end he handed me a cloth that smelled of something like kerosene and gestured that I should remove the ink. I rubbed and rubbed, but it did not come off and he looked at me with disappointment and waved his hand toward the door.

I looked back on the year of our discernment. I had thought at the beginning that it would be a matter of looking for signs or listening for voices, not too many steps away from divining tea leaves. But it had become a different matter. It had been as if I were invited into a slow stripping away to expose what lay underneath. Some aspect of myself or a part of the past would rise up, something left unattended and unresolved, to which I'd grown so accustomed I did not see it, like the low-lying tree branch in the backyard I instinctively duck. Often a person would bump into this long-held secret I kept from myself, sometimes by accident or as if by accident, and insist that I take a look.

A few months after our first conversation in his office, Mark Asman and I were sitting in a coffee house down the street from the church and he asked me, casually, about my college years.

"So where did you go to school?"

"St. John's."

"The one with the basketball team?"

"No, the one with the Great Books seminars."

I told him all about it: the Greek tutorials, the years of math and science, the seminars, the don rags, and the oral exams.

"Very impressive," he said. "So what's your degree in? Liberal Arts?"

"I didn't graduate," I replied, stiffly. "I left school at the end of my sophomore year. I was invited, or 'enabled' as they said there, to go on to my junior year, but I left instead."

"You don't have an undergraduate degree?"

"I don't," I said, "and I don't really care about that." And I started to cry.

"Well," he said, handing me a napkin. "Maybe we should try running that by again."

"You pretend to be completely together," he said gently, "not unlike another person I could name sitting here at this very table, but part of this process, I assure you, will be the dismantling of that carefully constructed persona."

I snuffled.

"Such an articulate person," he replied, calling for the check.

Once I'd unearthed a part of myself—like the pain and humiliation I felt over lacking a B.A.—immediately lots of other things would fall out of balance. I was like the old Volkswagen Beetle I'd had in my twenties that ran just fine until I tinkered with it. If I changed the oil or replaced the spark plugs then everything else, carefully poised in dysfunction, would let go.

The person who set off the dismantling was always the perfect person to hold on to while I came apart. The Holy Spirit, I began to see, was relentless, but she was not mean. Mark Asman went through a lot of Kleenex.

"If we come to terms with the reality of our past, and our present," Ann Jaqua said, "then we can ask what is being asked for the future."

In the midst of it all, I had discovered I loved preaching. The first, a homily on the Annunciation at the Thursday service at Trinity. Then, a homily at the monastery, right after Kit's death. On that day, Scott Richardson, the priest at St. Mary's Church in the little town of Lompoc, north of Santa Barbara, invited me to preach at his church, and we picked a Sunday service in Advent. I asked George Barrett for tips, especially on how he remained so calm before preaching, and he replied, "Librium."

A preacher in the Episcopal church usually preaches at each of the Sunday services and St. Mary's had two, one at 8:00 a.m. and one at 10:00. I live about forty minutes from Lompoc and so I rose that morning at six, in the foggy December weather of California, dressed and drove off—nervous, sleepy, and late. About a block from my house, I noticed a light on the dashboard, glowing orange. Gas! I said to myself, Oh, no, and then swung the car into the nearest station where I flung ten dollars at the attendant and plunged the gas nozzle into my tank. About thirty seconds later, gas poured out of the tank, onto the car, and onto my attractive wool skirt. I stared in incomprehension, and finally pushed the lever down to cut off the supply. Still not understanding what had happened, but by this time seriously late, I drove off, the attendant waving my change at me from the station door. About a block away, I noticed the orange light still on and then looked more closely at it. It was the indicator light for the rear window defogger that I had turned on myself that morning. The gas tank, of course, had been full.

When I arrived at Lompoc, the procession was just lining up, the organ was sounding. Scott placed a white alb over my head and as I struggled to put my arms through the sleeves, my sermon grasped in one hand, he sniffed at the cloud of gasoline wafting from me and whispered, "Better make a wide berth of the Advent candles."

I, who still cannot make a speech without becoming clammy and dumb, entered the pulpit at St. Mary's with a kind of singing joy. After the service, as people talked to me and urged me to go to seminary, I had a vision of them having a field to plow, nothing grander than that, and I was the one to plow it.

Discernment, I came to see, was about looking everywhere for traces of God. Noting the joy I felt entering the pulpit and the response of the people to my sermon. Noting the shame I had hidden in myself about not finishing college. Traces of God seemed to me to be marked by the discovery of an opening, like the hidden door in my dream, or what physicists call "worm holes," connections between, for want of a better word, realities. It seemed to be about revealing, shedding light, liberating. The Holy Spirit seeks to uncover, reveal, open. Nick, one of the monks at Mt. Calvary, said he once looked up from prayer one evening to discover that the colors in the chapel seemed brighter.

I was becoming alert to this shift, this sense of otherness, but I could not yet interpret it. Did the fact that I felt a shift when I preached mean that I should be a priest? Or could it mean, instead, that preaching was simply something I was "called" to do? Laypeople are allowed to preach in the Episcopal Church; a diocese may require a licensing of some kind to preach if one is not ordained but there is no church canon denying preaching rights to the laity.

The trap in this was to make it too literal, as Mark Benson would say. Or too literal too quickly. Where were Phil and Kit? At the zoo. What was I called to be? A zookeeper.

In between the application's questions, I weeded the rose garden. I looked down as I tapped on the keyboard at my nails that had dirt under them and I remembered one night at our base community. We read the story of Jesus at the wedding at Cana when Jesus is asked, at the last minute, to do something about the fact that they've run out of wine.

"I think this gospel is saying that we are asked to take something ordinary, like water, and make something extraordinary of it, like wine," Ann Jaqua said.

Very soon after that base community, Ann and I had gathered with three friends in Ojai and Santa Barbara to look at one another's gardens, offer advice on troublesome areas, and make more communal the solitary work of gardening. We called ourselves the Women's Gardening and Revolutionary Society.

We learned a lot about plants, and, of course, we learned quite a lot about soil. Plants grow best—we all know this—in rich soil that crumbles easily in the hand, black soil, full of abundant food. The best soil is compost, like that in my friend Corrie's garden in which she grew pole beans, ruby tomatoes, and summer squash. Corrie's compost came from wood shavings and sludge from Ojai's sewer plant. My friend Christina recommended coffee grounds for roses. Brother Roy, at the monastery, advised banana peels. My own compost was made of vegetable leavings, old oranges, corn husks, plants that had died in the garden, cut flowers past their prime. The soil that made the best garden growth was what was cast out. Plants grow best in garbage.

When I worked once a week in the soup kitchen at Trinity, the vegetables from which the soup was made were given to us by the produce manager at a local supermarket. He said to us when we came begging that he would give us his blemished vegetables and fruit (he has to clean out his bins every day) even though it was against the rules, because he couldn't stand to throw away good food. Thus we fed 125 people a day on Dumpster salvage.

Trinity had recently begun what is called a healing ministry: pairs of people, all of whom had training or experience in spiritual direction, were chosen by Mark to stand in a corner of the church and pray privately with anyone who approached them with whatever happened to be on their minds. The teams were often a mix of clergy and laity. At a brief "training," we had talked over the need for confidentiality. "You all know this," Mark said, "but let me just remind you, please, don't talk to anyone about what is said to you. Not your best friend. Not your spouse. And, further, you don't even mention it to the person who brought you the confidence, unless they bring it up. The whole thing remains in that space where you were in the church. Unless," he paused. "Unless the person speaks of wishing to commit suicide, or murder, or physical or sexual abuse. Then you must tell them that you are going to tell me. Okay?"

We had all nodded and I had felt the ante go up.

Mimi Simson, a laywoman trained as a sociologist and a spiritual director, had talked about how the whole thing might be about "movement."

"The person comes to you, and that's a movement, and then you move toward him or her. The Spirit moves in you to pray the right words. And then, they move back out, into the wholeness of being in community again."

We had not known what it would be like. I had been no more ready for the experience of serving communion than I had been prepared for this. What would I say? How could I rehearse? Right after communion, Ev Simson and I walked over to the corner near the pulpit and stood there, waiting. Our first "customer" was a beautifully dressed young woman, a visitor. She came toward us as if seeking a raft in high water. We held out our arms at the same time without having known we would do this, and made a little shelter with them around her.

She told us of her trouble in a forthright, strong voice. I was moved by her strength and her honesty.

I took a minute to think over what she had said but I didn't want to wait too long. "Gracious God," I began, and the words came out one after the other like a line of music slowly forming itself as it was played.

Ev pushed his thumb into the anointing oil and made the sign of the cross on the woman's forehead. "I anoint you," he said, "in the name of the God who made you. The Christ who gave his life for you. And the Spirit who sustains you every day." She looked at him, tears shining in the corners of her eyes, and then kissed him on the cheek.

"Thank you," she said. When she walked away, she stood taller than when she had approached us. She was moving back into the wholeness of community.

Jesus said to many of the people he healed, "Your faith has made you well." Her coming to us felt to be the beginning of her own healing.

In later weeks, they had come, one by one, and I had seen the reality of people's experiences, the reality of the congregation in a whole new light. I saw what was hidden in the people of the parish, all the suffering and anguish, and I felt what a great privilege it was to be there in the midst of them and their great courage. On those days, I felt as if I were part of some great cloud that was sheltering us in the church; the choir singing, the people moving, the ushers gesturing all seemed a long way away. With the prayer teams was this vast hand that joined with something in us making something bright, filling in our cracks, arousing our mercy, reaching toward those who came to us. When a priest wasn't there and I did the anointing myself, when I pressed my thumb into the oil and made the sign of the cross on their foreheads, I felt their skin under my skin and I looked into their eyes.

As I continued the application, I thought about those people who had come to us for prayers. I thought about the Gospel of the water and the wine. I thought about gardens and the soup kitchen, the joy of anointing with oil and preaching and how wonderful is the work of transformation. Wasn't it true that God constantly makes something out of nothing? Take a pregnant, unmarried woman; tax collectors; blind beggars; a son conceived out of wedlock. Take me.

In the compost made of old scraps, decayed matter, a new plant thrives and grows. In the kitchen, among homeless men and women, we'd had something I'd never felt anywhere else, something a friend called "radical serenity." During this process of discernment, I had seen the silent and steadfast work of transformation, not only in me but in others. In the water, was the wine.

In late May, a group of women from Trinity met at Terry Walker's house for dinner. Terry was then a business consultant, but she had recently decided to go back to teaching elementary school, having left it thirteen years before. She's a tall energetic woman with short graying hair in her fifties, with the long lean body of a swimmer. She regularly swims in the ocean, at dawn.

She served lasagna and a tossed salad that night, and after we'd eaten, Terry asked us to look under our plates for questions she put there, that she hoped we'd answer.

"Who was the most influential person in your life?" Terry Roof read from her slip of paper. She thought about it for a minute and said, "My father." Someone else said Eleanor Roosevelt. My mother. Hillary Clinton. Everyone except Terry Walker had answered by then and we looked at her expectantly.

"I will have to say it's Archbishop McIntyre," Terry said.

"Wasn't he the guy, isn't he the guy, who was bishop of LA?" asked Iva Schatz.

"He's the one," Terry replied.

"So why is he your person?" Iva asked.

"He changed my life," Terry replied.

"I was a nun," Terry said, "as many of you know, from 1961 to 1968. My order was the Sisters of the Immaculate Heart. In 1963, my community started to reflect in small groups on how effective we were being in our ministry. At about the same time, Vatican II invited all religious communities to examine their daily lives and see if anything blocked their ability to respond to the needs of the people they served. In our small groups, we became very much aware that our clothing and our rigid prayer schedule kept us from being with children and adults at times convenient to them. We didn't go out at night and our clothing often scared people away. In 1967, after four years of study, we decided to stop wearing the habit and to reschedule the daily offices of prayer so that we could be more available for our teaching and hospital ministries. We were the first community to make these changes and we got a lot of media attention. Our changes were not met with favor by the archbishop.

"I remember when I took off the habit," Terry continued. "I was teaching junior high in a Catholic school, with many secular teachers. I realized that when I wore the habit, I felt more 'holy' than the lay teacher down the hall. Without the habit, I felt as if I were the same as she was, no better, no worse.

"But soon John XXIII died, and a new regime took over at the Vatican. The archbishop of Los Angeles communicated his disapproval of the nuns' changes to Rome. Ratzinger sent three bishops to the United States to interview the 450 members of our order.

"I remember the one who interviewed me," Terry said. "He was a small man, with large hands. He was arrogant, and condescending. He called me, 'My child.' "

The bishop told Terry and the others that they must return to wearing the habit and the other customs or face dismissal from the Catholic church as a religious community. Only about fifty members of the community agreed to comply. The rest chose to continue as a lay community of women without the approval of Rome even though they had to find new work (they were fired from their jobs in the Los Angeles archdiocese) and new ways to do ministry.

Terry Walker left the Sisters of the Immaculate Heart community in December of 1968.

"And so I have to say," Terry said that evening, "that of all the people who influenced my life, it was Archbishop McIntyre who influenced it the most. Through his authority and recommendation, I was betrayed by the church I had given my life to."

"Women tend to love the church as if it were a human being," wrote the superior of Immaculate Heart. "This is a mistake. The church is an institution, not a person, and it will behave as an institution behaves."

As I listened to Terry, I had a sense of time slowly slowing down. More and more, she was in sharp focus and the rest of the room was blurred. The blue cotton cloth of her shirt and her face were luminous. And I thought, she is still a nun or, at least, a "vocation" is still calling. I wondered, How would it be seen again, how would it emerge?

As I drove home, I thought about the experience of the Sisters of the Immaculate Heart. If I were to be ordained, I would enter into a new relationship to the church. I would be an employee. The bishop would be my boss. I would have to make a vow of obedience to him. I had never agreed to obey anyone.

I finished the application. Then I sat and waited. Several years ago, a friend who went through the process was sent a letter from the Commission Ministry telling him that, in order to go forward, he had to complete certain tasks.

"Is this some kind of code?" I asked a monk at the monastery. "Are they telling him he should forget about it?"

"No," he replied. "If they meant that, they would send him an NFW letter."

"What's that?"

"No fucking way," he explained. "And they'd sign it, 'Yours in Christ.'"

Word came through the grapevine that there were twenty applicants for the ministry study year and twelve slots.

Phrases I had heard first in Nicaragua came back to me: *"Caminante, no hay camino"* (Seeker, there is no path). *"Se hace el camino al andar"* (The path is made by walking).

5

On June 30, I received a letter from the Episcopal Diocese of Los Angeles. The Commission on Ministry wanted to interview me for the ministry study year. There would be three interviews with members of the Commission on Ministry, each lasting about thirty minutes. The "conference," as they called it, would be held on Friday evening and Saturday morning, September 12 and 13. I was to send in a card confirming which day worked for me. The letter confirmed that there were twenty applicants for twelve slots.

The first institutional hurdle was crossed and I felt a mixture of triumph and anxiety. What would I say to them? Was I supposed to impress them with my sanctity? My intellect? My "call"? What would I wear?

Vincent and I went to the counselor once a week. In the first session she said, "If you can, I'd like you to turn to each other and say good-bye. If this is it, then see what that feels like."

I turned, and Vincent turned, and I felt a stone in my chest. I could not say it. He was crying. I saw our marriage as a separate entity, a third mysterious life between us, and we could kill it.

She asked us what we had thought about and I told her.

"It is a living thing," she said. "You made it together." Then she added, "But sometimes a marriage has to die, or the unconscious agreements in that marriage have to die, for another marriage, with the same partners, to come into being. I think sometimes that people start trying to kill the old marriage so that new marriage can arrive and end up just killing each other. We can have not one but many marriages in our lives, with the same person, if we can make it through."

She left us with some homework: "Don't try to talk about the priesthood or anything else that is hot right now," she said. "Don't talk about what you talked about in here. Try telling each other what you appreciate about the other at the end of the day. Three 'appreciations' each. It sounds corny, but try it."

"Do we take turns?" I asked. "Or does one do three all at once and then the other?"

She looked at me, as if for the first time taking my full measure, and said, "I think you'd better take turns."

We'd been living in an atmosphere of so much built-up tension and anger without reprieve that, as a friend said once, one more drop of coldness or passive aggression suddenly turned the whole mix to acid.

But that night we went home feeling slightly better, as if there were some possible help in the offing, and feeling at least that we did not have to solve this thing together, this thing we couldn't solve. Neither one of us wanted to be the one who started the "appreciations," but finally Vincent said, grumpily, "Shall we do the homework?" I nodded.

"I appreciate it that you made the appointment with Patty," he said. And I felt my heart fill, a small tide of something other than acid, an antidote. And the phrase from the bishop's letter about the women's ordinations came back to me: "walking in newness of life."

"I appreciate it that you changed a meeting in order to get there," I said. His face softened slightly.

"I appreciate . . . ," he said, and then we sat down, more humble and more appreciative, to dinner.

. . .

The next weekend, we joined friends from the Bay Area at an inn in Big Sur. Bill Glover was in training to become a Freudian analyst. Andra, his wife, my old roommate and friend, was a fundraiser for a large community-based medical care program in Berkeley. Seth worked in housing for the homeless in San Francisco, and Wendy, his wife, ran a successful physical therapy center and was thinking of going back to school to get her Ph.D.

The inn was an old place, with paper-thin walls and shared bathrooms and hearty food. Over bacon and eggs and fruit the first morning we were there, the conversation meandered from psychology to religion, the connections and similarities between the two, and the differences.

"I am wondering if a 'call' to the priesthood might be like the feeling I have about wanting to be an analyst, about feeling almost compelled to be," Bill said.

"Urban Holmes, an Episcopal priest, said, 'Once the priestly image has fallen upon an individual, it haunts them,' " I replied. "Does your wanting to be an analyst haunt you?"

"Sometimes in more ways than one," he said.

"Do you believe in the soul?" I asked.

"I'm not sure," he laughed, and stole a piece of his wife's bacon.

The next day we all hiked into the redwoods, and then Andra and I walked down to the water to sit near an old shipping dock.

Bill arrived and sat down in silence. Then he turned to me and said, "Maybe the soul is the thing in us that wants to go through all the pain and angst of analysis to find out about itself."

6

Just before the Commission on Ministry interviews, Vincent and I took a week off and drove to Yosemite. It was still early spring; waterfalls gushed from the great heights of the steep granite walls. The valley floor was crowded with Winnebagos, young women teetered on platform shoes, boy climbers carried bouldering pads on their backs to cushion a fall like beggars carrying mattresses, tourists in loud shirts photographed complacent deer, the Ahwahnee Hotel's lawns and terraces and long reading rooms stretched out in privileged lassitude. On the floor itself, we moved in a landscape so similar to Central Park—it was laid out by the same landscape architect—that it felt uncanny to see forests and granite walls just up ahead rather than the flags of the Plaza Hotel. On the other hand, a loud crash of falling ice reminded us that we were not in New York at all, but somewhere else, a place still rough and dangerous. It was at once wild and beautiful and painfully tamed. In the Yosemite Lodge's huge store, so stuffed with visitors you could hardly move down the aisles, everything from California wines to CDs were sold.

I felt a mysterious melancholy begin to seep into me, and I had strange, disorienting dreams. Gradually, I felt as if I could not find myself anymore. No matter what I did—walking, hiking, eating, napping, not napping—I felt out of sorts, displaced. I almost suggested to Vincent that we leave early; I felt as if the place were haunted by unhappy spirits. But toward the end of our week there, I went rock climbing with two old friends, both of whom had long been coming to the valley. As I walked toward our meeting place, carrying my climbing shoes with their sticky rubber soles around my neck, a bobcat burst through trees across a clearing and froze in stalking position.

When I placed my hands on the rock, my melancholy began to lift. And as we climbed upward, tracing a route with our hands and feet, moving over the ancient face, I felt that a way was being made for me to return to myself.

As Vincent and I drove home down Highway 99 through California's Central Valley where industrial agriculture has created a cesspool of pesticides, where the soil, as an organic farmer said to me once, is there just "to prop up the plants," I thought about how quickly the lethargy and depression had lifted from my heart once I was on the granite face. Part of that was the Zen-like state one must enter in order to successfully climb a vertical wall: there is nothing like the fear of death to focus the mind. And part was how something as difficult and as physically demanding as climbing almost always distracts the self from its concerns. But I had tried distraction earlier in the week, and it had not worked. It was more than what always happens to me when I climb rocks. I began to think about the places Native Americans name as sacred: Black Mountain in Arizona or Devil's Tower in Utah; Quskas in British Columbia (called Ellerslie Lake by whites), sacred to the Heiltsuk nation. We gringos don't know exactly how to think about this aspect of Native American religious culture—we tend to either swallow it all, whole, or cynically dismiss the idea of sacred places. But as we drove south, I thought, There is a way to comprehend sacredness of place that does not require us to take on another's religious shading. When he visited Ellerslie Lake the writer Rick Bass described the grace he felt there as having been given "a second chance."

"The natural world fits together," I recalled Ann Jaqua saying during our visit to the monastery. "It's one of those things that exceeds us in intelligence, freedom, and purpose. It can't be pinned down."

I had felt on Yosemite's ancient granite walls a "second chance," a measure of grace. I wondered if that was how Jesus affected those around him, those he healed. Jesus' disciples saw in him an extension of the holy, as if he were "the son of God." He must have been infused with what we might now call wholeness, or clarity, or something larger still: he must have participated in "resurrected life" long before he died. His ability to heal may have flowed from this reality. Christians call them miracles, and that word tends to shut down any discussion of them: they just *are*. And while we can't, finally, know exactly how Mary Magdalene was cured of her demons, we can ask, and we can compare our own experiences. We know how a person's presence can affect us, how a doctor's calm and clarity can help us find the strength to get well, how empathy helps us heal.

And we know, many of us, the effect of the natural world on our health and well being. In Yosemite's rough, centuries-old granite, there is a wholeness, a calm, an ancient, intricate freedom and purpose. A priest said once, "I want to consult all there is about who I am." Literally in touch with the granite, I was calmed, I was restored to myself, I was "consulting all there is." Theologians speak of pantheism, seeing God as nature, and therefore worshiping nature as God (or "panentheism," God *in* nature). But to go even further, stepping between these theories like stepping across tilting stones in a flowing river, Yosemite and other great wild places stand alongside Jesus as having restorative power, as participating in resurrected life. They are infused with holiness. They, too, are the Incarnation. And they are as capable of being destroyed by powers and principalities as was Jesus. Are they also as capable of resurrection?

7

On September 13, Ann Jaqua and I got up at 5:30 a.m. and drove toward Los Angeles as early morning commuters were just hitting the freeway. Ann steadied a coffee cup on her lap and I sipped tea. My ten-year-old silk jacket with a print of wild irises hung in the back seat. I wore a pair of pale grayish-green wide-legged pants. I hoped to convey an impression of stylish piety. We talked about Trinity and the upcoming marriage of Charles and Philip. Everyone in the parish was invited. Charles's children from a previous marriage were going to give him away.

We took the exit to Echo Park and approached the offices of the diocese when I had a sudden hankering for a Coke. My stomach required it. We drove past the office building and into the parking lot of a large supermarket. When I went inside most of the people were Latino, and I felt at home, as if in New Mexico. I bought a bottle of Coke, a box of crackers for now, and a package of red chili for later.

We drove through a gated entry into the basement parking lot. Inside the diocesan headquarters, it was still early in the working day. A young woman sitting at the reception desk greeted us as we walked out of the elevator and asked us to sign in. Around and about were a few priests in collars rushing importantly about like white rabbits.

I was ushered into a meeting room with a few other women and men in it, a coffee urn at one end and some cups. I realized as I went in the door that this was my competition for those twelve slots and looked at them with a mixture of what I hoped was earnestness and self-assurance. One of them, a younger woman with dark, short-cropped hair, looked back and smiled, and my heart wished her well before my ego got in the way.

Very soon, Nancy Larkin, in charge of "vocations" for the diocese, the wife of a priest, and a lawyer who had quit her corporate job to work half-time here, gathered us and handed us sheets with our schedules on them, and the name and number of our meeting rooms.

The next minute I was out in the hall, gripping the schedule of "Nora Gallegher" [sic], trying to find the right office. I found it just before the hour of 9:00 a.m.

Inside were two men. One of them introduced himself gently as Steve Nishibayashi and said he was a pediatrician. The other man was very big—his shoulders blocked half of the tiny office from view—and his manner gruff. He said his name was Jon and didn't mention his profession. Both were dressed in civilian clothes. Rumor had it that each committee would have a mixture of laypeople and clergy, but in this room there was no way to tell.

Jon started out. "What's your history in the church?" he asked.

"I began attending the Episcopal church with my mother when I was fourteen," I said stiffly. "I was baptized and confirmed when I was fifteen."

"What's your profession?"

I wondered whether he had read my application.

"I'm a writer."

"What do you write?"

"Books."

"About?"

"Faith."

I felt as if I were being grilled. Was Steve the good cop?

Just at that moment, Steve asked, "Tell us a little about your book. It's about Trinity, isn't it?"

I told him about the book I was finishing, how it had started as notes on my "spiritual life" and had become a manuscript that had recently sold to a respected publisher in New York.

"So you have a contract?" Jon said.

"Yes."

"Hmm," he replied.

Then, out of the blue, he said, "Tell me about your relationship to the Eucharist."

"I love the Eucharist," I said and almost cried. "It is the place where I can enter into the mystery of whatever this is all about. It's as if you take ordinary things, bread and wine, and the consecration pulls from them their mysterious life-giving core. It in turn calls out of us our own ability to give life, our own mysterious willingness to act on the part of others." I stopped.

Jon stared at me.

"I agree with you," he said, and his voice softened. "I know just what you are talking about." And I knew he was a priest.

Our half hour was up. They said good-bye to me, politely, gently. Jon rose from his chair and patted me on the back, which almost knocked me over, and I left.

I had fifteen minutes to regroup. I walked into our little meeting room and ran into the woman with the short dark hair.

"I just had the strangest time," I said.

"So did I," she replied.

"This guy Jon was in my group," I said. "He acted just like a cop."

"That's because he was a cop," she replied. "Jon Bruno was a football player and then a cop, and then a priest, and now he's the provost of the cathedral, here."

"Argh," I said. And we both went off to our second meetings.

In a somewhat larger office, crowded with books, were four people stuffed around a table. A woman whom I recognized as Carmen Guerrero, a priest and a member of the diocesan staff, gestured for me to sit down.

"Would you tell us a bit about your family?" she asked.

I told her about my father, now retired from the law, and my mother, who designed and built adobe houses in Albuquerque. I talked about Kit, and his death.

"Tell us a bit about how your brother's death informs your vocation," she said gently. "I lost my brother, too."

"When I was reading your application, I thought about a friend of mine who died of AIDS," said one of the people at the table, a pale mild man.

And then the three of us cried. It was a moment of such awkward sweetness in the midst of what I had thought would be more grilling, that I let myself really weep. Carmen handed me a Kleenex and took a pull from her covered commuter's coffee cup. "It's Coke," she said. "I disguise it as coffee."

"I wish I'd thought of that," I replied.

A young woman at the table, who was pregnant, said she worked as a psychiatric nurse at UCLA Hospital.

"What are your thoughts on lay ministry?" she asked. And we all four talked about the need for the church to pay much more than lip service to the ministry of people working in the world.

I realized I was enjoying myself when it was over.

"Good-bye," Carmen said. *"Adios. Vaya con Dios."*

I walked back to the room and on the stairs ran into the woman with the short hair again.

"Nora," I said.

"Kay," she replied.

"This one was really lovely," I said. "I liked this one."

"Who did you have?"

"Carmen Guerrero—"

"Carmen?" Kay stopped me. "She's supposed to be a bear!"

"She is a sweetheart," I said. Then, "We both lost our brothers."

And then we were off to the last session.

I had trouble finding the room in the "retreat center." The directions the receptionist gave me went like this: "Go upstairs, then straight across to the door next to the elevator, then through that door to a long corridor, go outside and then make a U-turn. . . ."

As I rushed into a hushed hallway, a dark man dressed in clericals who had been sitting on a bench rose to his feet.

"Anthony!" I said, recognizing Anthony Guillén, chair of the Commission on Ministry and rector of a small bilingual church in Oxnard, a warm and intelligent priest I had gotten to know after bringing the labyrinth to his parish.

"Shhh," he said, laughing and putting his arm around me. "We're not supposed to know each other. How are you doing?"

"It's not too bad," I said.

"Good," he said. "This last one will be fine," and he herded me through a door.

It was a beautiful room. One of five kept by the diocese for private or small retreats. Its windows were long and narrow and looked out on a courtyard. It was completely quiet and felt as if people had prayed there. It had a modern table around which sat two other people, a tall woman, who said she was a therapist, and another, friendly man who said he was also a priest.

We talked about being called by God, each of us in turn, as if this were a conversation rather than an interview. The therapist talked about how the atmosphere sometimes shifted in the room when she was working with a client and how she had come to feel that as the presence of something holy.

"It is as if the two of us, my client and I, because of our efforts, have made the ground sacred, have invited the holy to come in the door."

The priest talked about not liking being a priest all the time.

"It's incredibly hard," he said. "I don't always know that I can go on. I feel torn by different voices: being an administrator, being a confessor, a celebrant, a preacher, a mediator. Often I go home and fall directly into bed."

Anthony said he struggled to "grow" his church and to bring

together the Latinos who had joined up with the older and more entrenched white parishioners. "I sometimes feel like shaking my fist at God, just yelling at him," he said, looking over at me. "Or her."

The honesty of the conversation built on itself. It had a vast gentleness about it, as if the Holy Spirit were quietly holding us in her palm, turning us over now and then to take a small peek. Anthony reminded me of New Mexico, as had Carmen Guerrero, and I felt as if Kit's hand were there as well. Finally, I realized I felt safe.

Then it was over. They stood up and shook my hand and I left.

Ann was waiting for me in the courtyard. We left the diocesan offices and headed straight for a fancy fabric shop across the street from the La Brea Bakery, where first we bought chocolate cherry bread. I wolfed down a slice. I was surprised that I had not felt the need to present myself as someone other than who I was. I realized that had been my worst fear.

We drove to Santa Barbara to wait for a call from the Commission on Ministry. When we got to my house a message was waiting. It was from Anthony Guillén.

"I am very pleased to tell you," it began, and Ann and I hugged each other. We drove to Trinity, where Mark grabbed us both. "I just heard," he said. "You are in!"

He led us both to the library. "Now let's strategize," he said.

"Strategize what?" I asked.

"Where you will spend the ministry study year."

"I've let the diocese know I want to spend it at St. Mary's with Scott Richardson," I said.

"Congratulations," Mark said. "Do you think what you want is what you will get?"

"Well," I said, uncertain, "Scott let them know, too."

"This is the beginning of your life not being your own,"

Mark replied. "Your life now belongs, or at least a good part of it belongs, to the diocese. They will decide where you will go. We can have an effect, maybe."

I thought, He's been going through this for twenty-five years.

"How do they decide?"

"I think they throw dice," he said. "It's got to be a parish within a reasonable driving distance. So, from Santa Barbara, that would be either Lompoc"—I smiled—"or Oxnard. But that's Anthony's parish and he knows you. I don't think they'll put you there. Or Ventura, St. Paul's. Nice guy there. Or I suppose they could go as far south as Camarillo. . . ."

"Oh, no, not Camarillo," I said.

"What's wrong with Camarillo?"

"It's so, so suburban," I said.

"That's probably what Jesus said when they asked him to come heal some people in Samaria," Mark replied.

"Very funny."

"Al Smith is in Camarillo," Mark said, warming to his subject.

"Oh," I said.

"What do you mean, 'Oh'?"

"He's a very nice man," I said and stopped.

"I suppose you spent a lot of time with him and had long heart-to-heart talks and that's how you know all about him."

I stiffened. "I met him."

"Yeah?"

"I met him. Once. At the monastery."

"Ah, your vaunted intuition. You could do much worse than Al Smith."

"Well, we did do worse, here, at Trinity, that is."

"I will get you for that."

"So how do we have an effect?"

"It's fairly dicey," he replied. "We can't appear to be lobbying. Let me talk to some folks. Who do you know in the diocese?"

"No one," I replied.

"God," Mark said. "How did you get this far?"

On Sunday, Mark announced my new status to the congregation during the announcements and they applauded. I felt a little silly. Betty Bickel said to me after the service, "This seems just right."

Nancy Larkin let me know by email that "sometime later in September" I would hear where I was assigned and there would "probably" be a gathering at the diocese offices of "mentoring rectors" from the ministry study year parishes and "students."

"What am I going to do?" I asked Mark after the Sunday service. "Should I argue about it if they assign me someplace I don't want to go?"

We walked into the sacristy, past the closets that held what Mark now called the church's collection of "obnoxious chasubles."

"Sure," he replied, as we headed into the inner sacristy, and Mark began scrubbing out a chalice. "You'll be very popular with the diocese."

"Come on, I mean it. I want to go to St. Mary's. I know Scott. He wants me to work with him."

"That may work out," Mark said. "But they tend to assign you to parishes that are different from your home parish."

"St. Mary's is different," I said. "Well, sort of."

"Scott's not that different from me," Mark said as he tidied a drawer and checked the purificator pile for Tuesday's service. "I don't know why they can't keep it straight," he muttered. "There's a pile for purificators and a pile for corporals. A pile for purificators and a pile for corporals. You'd think they'd get that, don't you?"

Not waiting for an answer he said, "Let me tell you a story. Sit down."

I sat down in the little chair near the stone sink where we poured communion wine directly into the ground.

"When I left my first parish, which was in beautiful Santa Cruz, a church in Oroville asked me to come up for an interview. Now Oroville is a nice little town in Northern California, nothing fancy. I got up early the day of the interview so I could drive up there and check out the scene before I was to be interviewed. I drove through town. It looked nice enough. I got to the church. It was almost nothing from the outside, sort of fifties-modern. I was disappointed, but I thought it might be okay on the inside. I walked in. What I remember was it had red Linoleum tile. And blond plywood pews. And cinder-block walls. I thought, I could turn around and head out and they'd never know what happened."

"What did you do?"

"I stayed. It was four of the best years of my parish ministry."

"Point made," I said. "I will never like Camarillo."

"I never liked the Linoleum tile," Mark said as he walked past me into the church. Over his shoulder he said, "It was the people I liked."

On September 28 in the afternoon a couple of us were proofing the newsletter in the office, when the flowers began to arrive for Charles and Philip's wedding. It was hot, typical Indian summer heat in Santa Barbara, and the men who carried the flowers were sweating. A fan whirred softly in the corner of the office. Mark, immaculate in clericals, wiped his brow and alternately hovered and flitted, like a nervous butterfly, from office to parish hall to sacristy and back again. Then a woman walked in dressed in a bra top and white shorts, a tattoo of a rose on her left shoulder, with a young boy at her side. She was homeless, she explained, and they needed a room for the night. Mark told her he had arrangements with some motels and could write a check for a night's lodging. She could use the phone to call and find a vacancy and then he would write the check. The child, meanwhile, wandered into the parish hall.

She got on the phone in the copy room next to us, we continued proofing the newsletter, the flowers kept arriving. I felt it as a scene from some uncensored Brueghel: the flowers for the same-gender marriage, the homeless woman and child, the newsletter volunteers—all cheek by jowl, clicking along, toward Bethlehem.

Just as the woman said on the phone, "Do you take two-party checks?" for the third time, her child ran in from the parish hall and announced, "Mom! The wedding this afternoon is for two men!" I stopped reading the newsletter. The other editor froze in the midst of turning a page, one hand poised in the air.

I leaned back in my chair to get a good look. The woman was looking down at her son. She nodded.

"Okay, Andy," she said wearily. "We still have to find a room for the night."

In the sacristy, Martha Smith was ironing the linens. Her hands moved across the old ironing board that flipped down from the wall next to the processional cross.

"I will be coming to the, uh, ceremony," she said to Mark as he wafted out of the inner sacristy. "But—" And she stopped.

"But?" he said, turning, one hand on the ironing board.

"I will not come to communion."

"How come?" he said gently.

"Because I don't believe in this," she said softly, tilting the iron back to rest on its heel and smoothing the fair linen with her hands and then smoothing it again.

"That's okay," Mark said, putting a hand lightly on her shoulder. "Thank you for telling me. Just promise me one thing."

Martha nodded.

"Promise me you will come."

"I will," she said, and took the iron back into her hand.

Charles's grandchildren led the wedding march. Two little girls in frilly dresses. His daughter and son-in-law followed. Then several more grown children. All dressed up in suits and dresses, looking nervous and excited. Charles and Philip followed them, dressed up in blazers and smart ties.

The church was packed, and heads turned to see them come up the aisle, and I think probably each one of us was asking whether we felt, well, different, at this wedding than at other weddings. I felt the same tears coming as I always do when two people walk down an aisle with so much hope and promise in their hearts, engendering so much renewal of hope for others. These two were, like others I had seen before them, proclaiming the human gift of making a promise.

They stood up before Mark, and he said, "Dearly Beloved, we have come together in the presence of God to witness and bless the joining together of these two men in Holy Matrimony."

Then he said, "Charles, will you have this man, Philip, to be your spouse; to live together in the covenant of marriage? Will you love him, comfort him, honor and keep him, in sickness and in health; and forsaking all others, be faithful to him as long as you both shall live?"

"I will," Charles replied.

Mark led Philip through the same declaration, and Philip answered, "I will."

Anne Howard then rose to preach.

"We stand today on new ground," she began. "It is a new day. We have never been here before, and it's a little scary."

She talked about listening to Charles and Philip talk about their histories. "I know," she said, "that the road to this place has been marked by struggle."

Then she told a story.

On our visit to England five summers ago, my husband Randy, and our son Ben, and I . . . went to Durham . . . to see the shrine of St. Cuthbert, the seventh-century monk famous for his healing powers. We entered the cathedral, pulling open the huge heavy door with a huge brass lion's-head door knocker. I was not ready for what was inside. . . . Massive columns of stone carved eight hundred years ago rose up around me. A mighty fortress indeed. The whole place spoke of power, frankly, the power and might of Norman kings more than the holiness of God.

And then I looked down at the floor. . . . I looked down and saw a long, wide black marble line inlaid in the stone floor. It stretched across the entire width of the nave, across the back end, the west end. I had never seen anything like it. And then I looked up and saw a framed sign posted on the column, explaining the line. The sign said the marble was laid there in the 1100s, when the cathedral was built, to keep the women back, to keep the women away from the main part of the church. It was a protective barrier, to keep the altar and St. Cuthbert's holy shrine pure and free from the corrupting power of women. . . .

It hurt to see that line. It hurts to remember it even now—that barrier established in the name of purity. That day, as I stood there, surrounded by the power and might of the church, I thought of the men who had laid that marble and all the women who had stayed behind the line. . . . We all know about lines. . . .

That line on the floor of Durham Cathedral serves no purpose anymore. It is a relic from the past. I believe that the day that marble was laid, God wept. And I believe that every time we cross a line like that, God dances.

Today, we cross the line. Today, old barriers lose their power, old wounds can lose their sting. Today, as we gather our collective courage and our good will, healing is possible because we gather to celebrate something larger than ourselves.

Today we celebrate not only the love of these two men but the love of a God that invites all of us to cross the line, to stay back no longer, to step into healing, and into hope and into joy.

Today, we cross that line. And so today, God is dancing. Amen.

She sat down. The church was as quiet as a deep forest. We sat there, in the quiet, and then Charles and Philip stood up and exchanged their vows.

And after we had wished one another the peace of God, and after we had sung a hymn, and after Mark and Anne had co-presided at the Eucharist with all of us joining in, we began communion. We had stations for communion: a priest and two chalice bearers at the head of the church, right near the altar, on either side. I stood up and joined the long line of people to eat this bread and drink this cup today, and after I had taken communion, and sat back down, something made me look up. And down the aisle in the communion line came Martha Smith, solemn, quiet, measured.

She crossed herself and reached her hands up when she arrived in front of Mark and opened her palms like a crane coming to rest in water.

"The Body of Christ," Mark said, placing the bread on her uplifted palm.

"Amen," she replied.

.   .   .

And when we were all finished, the two men knelt in front of Mark as he said the final blessing. It was clear Mark was only barely keeping his own tears at bay.

"O God, the giver of all that is true and lovely and gracious: We give you thanks for binding us together in these holy mysteries. . . ." Then he leaned down and drew their heads together with his large hands and held them tight and close. Then it was over and the congregation sang the final hymn and they strode down the aisle hand in hand.

Afterward, in the sacristy, Martha Smith was cleaning the chalices and placing the linen in the laundry bag hanging by a hook near the door.

Mark came in from the church, and he saw her there, going about her Altar Guild business, matter-of-factly, solemnly. She looked up at him and he looked at her.

"May I ask you, Martha, why did you come to communion?" Mark asked. "If it is any of my business at all."

"Because I've drawn too many lines in my life," she replied and held his gaze for a second or two, and then she reached down and picked up another chalice to wash.

In the parish hall for many hours, we danced.

The next day, I got a letter announcing that I was assigned to Camarillo, the Reverend Al Smith, rector.

THE HOURS
OF THE SPIRIT

⤬

1997—1998

1

As I drove south, I realized I was repeating the phrase "What am I doing here?" over and over in my mind until it was becoming a mantra. I had driven beyond Santa Barbara's lovely, privileged architecture, past the beachside cottages that mark its border, and into the land of ranch houses and strip malls. "What am I doing here?" I said, as chain restaurants, built in plundered citrus and avocado orchards and called by the names of fruits, flowed by. As I passed another Home Depot, I remembered those lines in the Book of Exodus muttered by the Israelites as Pharaoh's army closed in on them: So, Moses, they said. You brought us to the wilderness because there weren't enough graves in Egypt?

It was Wednesday evening. I was going to meet Al Smith, my new rector, at his church and attend an education committee meeting as their new ministry-study-year student.

There were twelve of us, a scriptural number, in that year's ministry study year program, half women and half men, ranging in age from nineteen to sixty. We would each spend a year in a parish other than our sponsoring parish, working with a new priest and another discernment committee. (We would occasionally spend a Sunday or two in our "home" parishes.) During this year we would be examined by a psychologist hired by the diocese and take the Minnesota Multiphasic and other psychological tests designed to root out psychopaths. At the year's end we would be interviewed, again, by the Commission on Ministry and, if all went well, we would become "postulants." Three years of seminary followed, more interviews, and finally ordination.

Our group of ministry-study-year students would meet once a month with two mentors: a priest and a layperson. David Duncan was the priest, a tired-looking man, father of two toddlers, who was holding down this job and another as interim rector at a small parish south of LA. Ann Jaqua was the layperson. We would read papers assigned by our mentors, write four papers on various topics, and check on how things were going in our new parishes. Our group had met for the first time at the diocesan headquarters in Los Angeles around a long table in the bishop's meeting room.

That day, Saturday, a business day in the church, the bishop, Fred Borsch, was working in his office next door. I had looked around the table and seen some of the people I remembered from the day of the interviews with the commission: a large woman in a green jumper, a young neat boy in jeans who fell asleep halfway through the session, a nervous woman with dry blond hair. To my immediate right was Kay, the woman I'd spoken to on that interview day, wearing a white T-shirt and khakis, her hair in a neat, boy's short cut. There we were, jars of water, brimful of possibility, waiting.

We were supposed to tell the story of how we got here, and I was trying to think of something short and profound when a guy who was slouching in his chair spoke up.

"It's simple. God called. I ran. I lost." He stopped speaking, a satisfied smile on his face. David Duncan looked up and said, "Is that it, ah," and he consulted a sheet on the table in front of him, "Ken?"

"Well, yeah," Ken replied. "I mean, yeah."

"Okay," David said quietly and peered over his glasses at the rest of us. "Someone else?"

The woman sitting next to me cleared her throat. "Kay Sylvester," she said in a deep voice. She worked for something called Volleyball One in Huntington Beach. She said that among other things she bought and sold wrestling equipment. Kay said she was a recent convert to the Episcopal church, having grown up in Colorado in an Evangelical church. She said she had been hurt badly by that church, did not elaborate, and said she left it in her twenties. When she moved to the Los Angeles area, her best friend, Lucy, invited her to church. Kay sat in the back for many months, "annoying Lucy with questions: Why do you kneel? What's the priest doing with the bread and the cup?" When it came time for communion, all the others rose and walked forward to receive it, but Kay sat still with her arms crossed.

"After a long time, maybe six weeks, the rector of the church came to me after church with his hands on his hips and his glasses pulled down to the end of his nose. He peered at me and said, 'Why don't you come to communion?' in a tone that implied I was missing something. I mumbled something like, 'I don't know,' to which he replied, 'This is our family, and this is our table. You should come.' I was hugely taken aback by his notice. It never occurred to me that I was the only person not coming forward to receive, that I stood out so vividly. His analogy to the family appealed to me but I don't think I went to communion the next week either.

"But Lucy finally said to me, 'What are you afraid of?' And this stung me. I had to act unafraid. So I went and I knelt and watched as the priest came closer and closer with a little silver bowl full of disks of something resembling Styrofoam. It was at this point that I realized I would have to open my hands. When the moment came, I came as close as I ever have to hearing voices. I heard an almost audible, 'Come on, girlfriend, open your hands.' "

Everyone had a story; none as wonderful to my ears as Kay's. One of the women had actually seen a vision of Jesus on the beach. I could feel the pressure to come up with a convincing line about God's call to me, as if it had been sent by FedEx.

I finally mumbled that I had found myself drawn to the altar and to the Eucharist because it was mysterious and had "no economic value," and I felt myself putting on that old and awful persona that was mine in high school, the rebellious, embittered smart-ass.

I had wanted to say something about the depth of my longing and my ambivalence, that the two seemed evenly matched, but it felt as if most of us were trying to prove to each other in this small room next to the bishop's office that ours was the one true call. I didn't want to play that game, but I played it anyway, because I could not bring myself to reveal my real heart, unlike Kay, or my real experience. Now I understood, I wanted to say, why most of the prophets had ducked.

Ken was from a conservative, Evangelical church in Orange County. He had been assigned to a liberal church. Kay had been assigned to St. Paul's in Tustin, where she was working with a woman priest. Ryan, the youngest at nineteen, was from a conservative parish and was working with a younger priest in a more liberal parish. The diocese had tried, I could see, to match us with parishes that were different from our homes, and rectors who might be new kinds of priests.

I had just met Al Smith at an ill-conceived breakfast hosted by the diocese. He was walking toward the elevators in the parking garage as I got out of my car. An athletic man in his early sixties, a runner and biker with a stiff set to his jaw, he'd been rector at St. Columba's for twenty-five years—too long in anyone's book, including his own. He was set to retire in a year; I was his last diocesan project.

We were like two people on a bad blind date as we sought desperately for common ground in the long, long walk to the elevator.

"Was the drive down okay?" Al asked.

"Yep," I said. "Got up a little early, but okay."

"Oh, I get up around five anyway, most days, so it wasn't too early for me."

"Oh, ah. Nice in the early morning?"

"Always quiet."

We reached the elevator and only then did I realize that we would now have to ride together, alone, in that small box, for God knew how long.

The door slid shut.

"Do you know how long this meeting is supposed to last?" Al asked.

"No," I replied. A long beat of silence.

"Well, I hope it's not too long," he said.

"Me, too."

The doors slid open.

We had decided at that meeting, which lasted longer than anyone wanted it to, that Al and I would work out a "contract" for the year, written down and signed. The diocese was not clear about exactly how many hours a week ministry-study-year students were supposed to work or what exactly counted as "work." Did the drive to the church count? Was Sunday worship added in? How about the study group meetings with David Duncan and Ann Jaqua? Sermon preparation time? We were all driving at least thirty miles to the new parish, and some of us were driving several hours to the monthly meetings. None of this work was paid and all of us were holding down jobs. When I and other students asked these questions or any question regarding the arrangements put forth by the diocese, we were greeted with a split-second hesitation that floated in the air like a piece of soot. I saw in those first weeks that we were in something as traditional as the prayer book, the boot-camp model of initiating the new.

. . .

As I pulled into the parking lot at St. Columba's, next to Al Smith's old black Honda, I noticed that there were no lights on in the parish hall. I got out of the car and began walking uncertainly toward the church when a little girl carrying a flashlight opened the front doors. I made my way toward her and introduced myself.

"The power went out," she said. "Father Al is in the back. Would you like me to walk with you to find him?"

I said I would.

Inside, in the dark, lit by only the light of this child's flashlight, the church actually looked not beautiful, not Gothic as did Trinity, but not bad. The blond wood of the pews, which in daylight looked like fifties TV cabinets, gleamed softly in this sweeter, more forgiving light. The cross, which was not a cross but a figure (not quite male, not quite female), holding out its arms over the altar, looked welcoming. In the shadows, there were two small alcoves, one for the choir and one for a chapel-like area, with a columbarium, a vault for interned ashes. It reminded me in this half-light of those older alcoves in the cathedrals in Europe where I had seen women wrapped in black shawls praying to the Virgin.

I would have liked to pray to the Virgin right then and there. I felt in exile, an imposter. Removing a candidate for the priesthood from her home church made sense to me. To properly "test" a person's ability to lead, it seemed right to check them out in a new setting for a substantial amount of time, but to test a "vocation" this way was not necessarily right. Priests in the early church rose up out of their community, were meant for that community, made of the same DNA. To remove us from our birthing places seemed unnatural, and might diminish the common good. If homegrown leaders ended up leaving, how did that serve those who remained?

But I was here, I realized, as I followed the child with her light, to find out my vocation, and exile was part of every myth, every journey.

Al Smith was working in the sacristy, a neat room behind the altar area with closets set into the walls, a standing cross, a desk, and one chair. Next to it was a bathroom, and then a hallway containing choir robes on one wall, and then the inner sacristy where the fair linens, hosts and wine, and chalices and patens were kept, with a sink for cleaning up. It was all done in the same fifties blond wood, a long way from Trinity's Gothic stone and dark pews. I wondered aloud where they got rid of the chalice wine after communion and Al pointed to the rose garden outside.

Using Al's flashlight, we left the church and went into a low building next door, the parish hall, with ubiquitous folding chairs and tables, a huge kitchen with a pass-through. Peering through the gloom, I could see at the far end large draped objects and an American flag. We walked through a door to a small office, where five people were sitting with flashlights and pale eyes. Al introduced me to Sylvia and Dennis, an elderly couple. "Like Dennis the Menace," he said with a big smile that widened his round red cheeks, while his wife looked at me with skepticism. "We're old and getting older," she said. The other couple were Colleen and Larry, Al said, turning to a woman with dark hair and dark beautiful eyes and her calm, kindly looking husband. Colleen worked as a nurse in a nearby hospital and Larry at a nearby naval station. Bob, a large friendly man at the end of the table, was the chairman of the committee. He said his daughter was starting out as a writer in the Bay Area. Al suggested to the group that they work with me on planning a Lenten series. They looked at me and I looked back at them. None of us knew exactly what I was supposed to be doing there. And from two of them, there was a look of . . . respect? As if I were . . . holy? Or at least, holier than they. I wanted to scream. I wanted to say, "This afternoon I threw the finger at a driver who cut me off on the freeway." I wanted to say, "I've forgotten how to pray. The ministry study year has taken up so much time, I don't have time to pray." But they didn't want or need to hear any of this. As I sat down, what a friend said moved through my mind.

"You are the material," my friend Christina had said. "They will use you."

2

Every Fourth of July until she died, I visited my great aunt Eugenia in Tryon, North Carolina. She lived in a little wood-paneled house that had simple, clean lines. It was designed by her architect husband, my great uncle, and was the guest house of the larger house up the road they had lived in with their two children. We would sit outside on the terrace, she in her wheelchair and I in a lawn chair, sipping gin and holding sparklers while the fireflies swam in the grass. She was in her late nineties when I first started visiting her. Aunt Eugenia had all of her faculties.

"What human attributes would be relevant or present in a hero, do you think, honey?" she said one evening as we sat outside.

And, "Tell me again, is 'proclivity' a word? What does it mean?"

"Tendency," I replied.

"Oh, yes, that's right. Now let's talk about natural selection. What I remember about it is that Darwin visited an island where different kinds of birds had different bills that could do different things. Now, where was that island, and does natural selection have anything to do with finding the right mate?"

She was slowly going blind—she watched TV about two inches from the screen—but one Sunday when we were watching David Brinkley she asked me suddenly, "Does Cokie Roberts have a new hair-do?" I looked carefully and replied that yes I believed she did. "We can't do without her," she replied. She smoked Camels in the evening, did not inhale, and the ashes collected along the ledge of the screen. When she was a hundred years old, she said to Vincent, "I really ought to quit smoking." And he replied, "Aunt Eugenia, whatever for?"

Eugenia would put me up in a nearby bed-and-breakfast and arrange my meals at a different restaurant every night. She would tell me where I was going to eat, and then, unbeknownst to me, call ahead and pay for the meal. The first time this happened I thought someone in the restaurant had taken a spontaneous liking to me.

One Saturday morning I ventured over to the next town, a little place with a bunch of small Victorian-era houses, a historical society, and an Episcopal church with a white bell tower. I was hungry and I walked into a place next door to a vacant lot called the Wildflower Bakery. There were round tables covered with magazines and newspapers, an old pew serving as a bench along one wall, and orders hanging from clothespins on a line. Someone had strung a circle of yellow leaves on a round lace doily like a wreath. Three women covered in flour were in the back behind a counter. One of them was wearing a cap that said "Chicago," and she came forward and I looked at her and she looked at me and we both burst out laughing. Then she wandered away without taking my order. I stood there for a while and then she came back.

"I have some cookies," she said, "but I haven't had time to put them out."

"I love it here," I said.

"You do?" she said, and wandered off, bringing me back a ginger cookie and waving away my money.

A woman rode up on a motorcycle, and walked in. She was wearing a purple shirt and a long red braid.

"LAUNDRY lady," all three women in the back yelled out.

Several more people came in, including a tall guy wearing a blue Oxford shirt and a wide smile. He sat down at one of the round tables and said loudly, "I just heard a great country-western song."

"How does it go?" said the woman behind the counter.

"Jesus loves me," the man sang out. A beat of silence.

The women cocked their heads.

"And he can't stand you."

As I sat in the bakery, reading, I hoped heaven would be like this.

The next morning I went to the little Episcopal church and when the time came to wish each other peace, I turned around and there he was, the guy with the song.

"Peace," he said and smiled.

"Jesus loves me . . . ," I replied. "And . . ."

"Oh, Lord," he said. "So you were there yesterday." He turned out to be the son of an Episcopal priest.

When I first found my way back to the church, I was not sleeping very well. I was afraid to go to movies because in theaters I sometimes had serious anxiety attacks. I could barely travel. I was twenty-eight, and I worked way too hard and drank way too much, and did just a little bit of cocaine. I woke up one morning and decided, for a little pick-me-up, I would do some cocaine, just to wake up. Just as I was lowering my nose to the rolled up dollar bill, I looked up and there before me was a mirror. I saw a very tired, very scared young woman with her hair in her face lowering her nose to a line of white powder. I put down the dollar bill and swept the powder into my hand and walked to the toilet and let it fall in.

The next day, I went to church for the first time in ten years. I picked a little church in Pacific Heights because it was small and made of wood and had low-carved beams. The preacher that morning, a small man with a balding pate, talked about how as a gay man he did not believe for a very long time that Jesus loved him. I sat in the pew and cried. I didn't know it then—it took hearing that country-and-western song title many years later—but I was sure that Jesus loved him but couldn't stand me.

A few weeks later, I managed to call the priest and make an appointment. I walked into the tidy church offices which were upstairs, down a hall, past a choir room, and finally into a little corridor that ended in a tiny office that was neat as a pin. Bill Barcus, in his collar and suit, rose to greet me. I think I started crying right away. I told him I was having an affair with a married man, and had just met one of this man's friends, a younger man, and that I liked him. I told him that I had recently broken off with a man who was witty and mean, that he had told me he thought he wasn't good for me and then had asked me for a girl-friend's telephone number. And he didn't iron the backs of his shirts, only the fronts, I added, and Bill laughed. Then I said I'd gotten involved with the married man and now I had met his friend. I was poor, I said, and deeply confused.

"Tell me a little about the men," Bill said. I went on about them, describing them, and feeling an odd relief in this, that he didn't seem the least bit shocked, only interested in the details, and I stopped crying.

He said, "They all seem quite different. It's good, I think, that they are different. If they were all the same, it would be some kind of repetitive thing, but these men are all quite different."

I looked at him and smiled. I felt a little tiny bit of hope. Bill Barcus then left the office for a minute and came back with a red Book of Common Prayer. "Keep this," he said, "and come back and see me next week."

When I went to see him I was so tired I fell asleep in the sec-retary's office. The first thing Bill said was, "Why don't you take a vacation?"

"I can't," I said. "I don't have any money."

"Take this," he said, pulling out his wallet. "Here's my credit card. You might really like Yosemite." I think Bill must have made less than $15,000 a year.

I broke up with the married man. Or rather, I let it go, as it was not made of much to begin with. I saw him, later, as the friend he was, and the advisor, the father-figure I needed to have. The younger man and I began to have lunch. Around once a month, one of us would call the other, and we would have uncomfortable, jittery lunches. Once we even went to Julius Castle, a stuffy restaurant perched above the bay, and sat at a table with a white cloth feeling self-conscious around the snooty waiters, but liking the view. We had gone to the same college, to St. John's, at different times, as it turned out, and because St. John's is such a small school, we had many friends in common. And because it's such a strange school, we felt like members of a small club. He had quit, too, after only a year. We talked about ideas mostly; I was alternately pleased with myself in his presence, and tired of myself talking. I was afraid to show him anything of how I felt. I did not want to fall in love again; I did not want to set myself up for a belittling, terrifying relationship in which I would let myself get hurt all over again.

I went to church every Sunday. I moved out of my lonely apartment and into a friend's house in the country, while she spent the summer in Chicago. All around me grew California bay trees, and below me was the sweet sound of a rushing creek. I stopped drinking so much. For days and days, I didn't drink at all. I wrote in the mornings and walked with the dogs in the afternoons. I drove across the Bay Bridge to go to church.

I went on having strange meals with the younger man. After four months, he called one day and said he wanted to have lunch. I thought that what I needed to do was tell him that it wasn't working for me, this way, dragging it out. It's too much for a friendship, but we can't seem to make the next move. A friend agreed. "Get it over with," she said, "like a cold shower."

As I drove, I thought about how I should say it, feeling a hollow ache—enough is enough, we're not going anywhere, it's too much for me—and I got to the restaurant and parked. It was a fish restaurant, kind of a touristy place, down near Fourth Street by the freeway in Berkeley. I went in and he was already there, and I sat down and ordered fried oysters, and he ordered a Bombay gin and tonic with bitters and patrole sole. The food came and I ate and talked and told him how the dogs were doing, thinking all the time I should just do it now, like a cold shower. He seemed distracted. We finished, and I thought, Now, and he said, "Do you want to go for a walk?"

"A walk?" I said.

"Yes," he said. "Somewhere around here. Let's just go for a walk," and before I could say anything he got up and paid the bill and started walking toward the door.

I followed him and we walked across the parking lot and across a street and then under the freeway, and onto a little littered beach. Old yellow sea ropes lay around on the muddy sand. We picked our way around a dead seagull. We could see the towers of San Francisco off in the distance. He walked for a while without saying anything and I thought I really should get this over with, and then Vincent turned to me and said, "I don't really like dating. Let's just get married and work backward from there."

We moved in together in a week and a half and lived together for almost two years, and then Bill Barcus officiated at our wedding under a hot sun in Sonoma, and we drank champagne and ate homemade chocolate mousse and swam in a pool and circle-danced outside all afternoon. One of my friends said, "It was so obvious to me that this was the man for you, and you were the woman for him, that I think you both spent seven months fighting it."

We moved to Colorado, and I fell into a church that met in

a back room in a restaurant. I was slowly crawling along toward Jesus.

I still had a hole somewhere that the drugs and the drink and the work had tried to fill, and I kept that hole protected, as if in a little horror museum of my own, in order to preserve my relationship to my past. But loving Vincent and being loved by Vincent set up another place in me, as if we were building an alternate place from which I could view the world—a guest house, if you will, of that large and ugly museum.

Kit was drinking heavily in New Mexico. He had yet to meet Rande, yet to find his surveyor's job. One weekend he called and said he was going to drive up and see me with a friend and arrived at four in the morning, smelly, muttering something about losing the directions. They left a few days later in the same dazed state and I couldn't figure out why they had come. It wasn't until after he died that I realized he had just wanted to see me.

In Colorado, Vincent and I lived in a small geography, far away from California. I noticed I felt a sense of relief growing in me as I went about my days, writing in the morning in the old porch of our log cabin, stoking the fire in the wood-burning stove, walking with Vincent's dog in the afternoons. I felt accomplished just getting through the day. I did not worry so much about my hair and my skin and whether or not I was fit enough and whether or not I was up on the latest healthy diet or the latest in self-help advice. Even though I had made fun of narcissistic self-improvement when I lived in California, I had not realized until I was removed from it how much I'd breathed it in. Just as it lifted from me, I understood that in California we were all trying desperately to perfect our lives (just one more ginseng colonic would do it!). But in this little string of towns and suburbs lined with pine trees and potholes no one had the time, the money, or the energy for that. Digging out our driveway after the winter's first blizzard, bringing in pine logs, and keeping the small woodstove going were accomplishments. On the weekends, Vincent and I listened to *Prairie Home Companion* and planned small excursions along the South Platte River. At the church, because we had no building and very little overhead, we gave away most of our money to the outreach committee. We made a deal with the local energy company that they would call us if someone couldn't pay a heating bill. I walked back and forth between church life and married life; the combination was simple and satisfying.

After the first few Sundays I'd been there, St. Columba's began to remind me of that Colorado church. Camarillo is not fashionable: it's made of outlet malls and chain restaurants and flat, ranch-style housing. The people at St. Columba's worked at the two local hospitals or in computer technology or at the nearby naval station. They dressed in clothes from Wal-Mart or Target. When I mentioned that sometimes I shopped at Barney's (New York) Outlet, they looked shocked. In the first weeks there, I felt shy at the coffee hour and my conversation openers about the weather grew thin. I began to place a few people: Marty, a young man who wore Coke-bottle glasses, limped badly, and was sweetly adoring; Marty's mother, Jane, who looked after her adult son; Colleen and Larry and Dennis and Sylvia. I grew to like and respect the associate priest on staff, Carri Patterson Grindon. I didn't really know how to "present" myself or how to bring to bear on the ministry study year my own complex past. I found myself head to head with the idealized image of a priest. My new discernment committee met the first Sunday I attended services in a little room off the parish hall, in which were stored old crosses, Sunday school materials, a flag, and an odd collection of wrought-iron ivy leaves. Batie, Bill, David, and Judy. They looked to me to be suburban: careful haircuts, nondescript clothing; people, I said to myself, who lived stable, humdrum lives. How was I going to relate to them? Batie was one of the church secretaries at St. Columba's. She had a cheerful, round face and a lot of intelligence in her flashing eyes; David, gruff, bearded, wary, was retired from the navy; Judy, tall, intelligent, was the principal of a K–6 school; and Bill—there was something wounded about Bill—was an electronics design engineer. We talked over lukewarm coffee. I asked them to tell me a little about their lives.

Batie said she had just seen her son, who came to visit. "He's twenty-five," Batie said. "It's been ten years," she continued, "and we said to each other last week, we can say we survived." My ears went up and I wanted to ask what this was about, but she looked away.

David said he had graduated from the Naval Academy and served twice in Vietnam, and still wondered how he had walked through a battlefield without getting hit.

After a few seconds, Judy said she was dealing with some pretty complicated issues at her school. The mother of one of her students had separated from her husband because she was in love with another woman. Oh, oh, I thought. The kids were having trouble in school. Judy sort of mulled it over in front of us. Was it because the mother was a—a split second passed before she said it—a lesbian? Or was it just divorce? All three of them looked at me.

"Our priest at Trinity is gay," I said. And let it sit for a minute. Then I said, "I think we are all wading around in this deep water to try to figure out how to do the right thing." Judy smiled and said, "It may just be that I don't think much of her new partner, whatever sexual preference she is."

"Well," I said, "I hope you keep bringing this issue back here to us. I would rather talk about all of our lives than just mine."

"That's a deal," she said.

Bill said he was the son of a priest, had grown up "poor but moral." Then he said, "My little boy died and is buried over there," and gestured toward the church and its columbarium.

"Why are we here?" David asked.

"Maybe we are called to be here," I replied.

David looked at me as if taking stock of a fresh recruit.

"Yes," he said, "but I meant what is it exactly we are supposed to be doing?"

I took another look at them. What does it take, I thought, to stop that split-second judgment, that early take, on someone? Why do I continue to get it wrong? Each of them had a story, and a life, and some of the stories were pretty hard if the hints bore out. Their lives weren't humdrum; the real concerns of the day had reached into this suburb as much as anywhere else.

In the next weeks, people in pain fell out of the sky.

In Encino, a lush, wealthy suburb of Los Angeles, I led a retreat on the labyrinth at a Roman Catholic convent built around a man-made lake complete with ducks. Built in the sixties, it once housed a hundred or more novices in twin-bedded rooms set around an inner court, but now only a few nuns lived there. They did a booming business, however, in retreats; ours was packed. Most of the women who had signed up were Catholic. One of them, a sexy woman who wore dark reds and silks, asked me to walk with her around the grounds. As we drew near the ducks, I realized she was making a confession, to a woman, to the closest thing she had to a woman priest. It was a story a woman would hear and understand and I was pleased to be there, to listen, as a woman, but I wished for anointing oil and the right to use it, to seal her forehead.

Part of my ministry-study-year agreement was to check in with the folks at St. Columba's who ran what they called The Pantry, a grocery give-away set up in the parish hall once a month. I drove down on a Tuesday afternoon and found long tables on which sat boxes of cereal, vegetables, and staples—cans of tuna, oranges, bananas, baby food. Volunteers were packing them into brown bags for pick-up later that day. After I flunked Bag Packing 101 by putting bananas on the bottom of a bag, they put me to work sweeping the floor.

One of them told me that a young couple and a child had come in the week before. They were, he said, "Hungry. As hungry as I have ever seen anyone come to The Pantry."

The people in pain formed a collection of experience: they seemed part of a larger discernment, as if I had been not only thrust out of my own congregation but out into a wider experience of the world. There were so many of them that, of course, I could not fix them. I served as a witness to pain's austerity, its ongoingness, and the way it was hidden in the lie of self-perfecting California. It was as if the prayer ministry I'd done at Trinity was now extended, its horizon deeper and broader.

Al Smith and I took a morning at Mt. Calvary. We sat in the south library, drinking tea and eating cookies that Robert Hagler brought us. We had not talked much or seen each other very much since our first odd breakfast encounter and I was nervous. We had decided to meet to talk about our stories. Al began. He said he wanted to tell me about his first job. Oh, Lord, I thought, spare me a litany of jobs.

"Okay," I said brightly.

He was fresh from seminary and had been sent by his bishop to Steven's Village, Alaska, a community of 180 Athabascan people, most of whom were Episcopalian. The year was 1959. In 1959, I thought, all the priests were men and priests were "sent" by their bishops.

"As I look back at that period in my life, I see myself as a young, inexperienced, fearful, immature priest," Al said. My ears perked up. "It was tragic because I could have had a rich life with the people of Steven's Village, since they poured out their hearts to me in their most quiet way and I wasn't prepared to accept their wisdom." Al sipped his coffee and spoke again. He said that as the fall approached, he started "turning inward." His depression grew as the winter days began, dark and cold.

"It was Monday morning in mid-January when the mail plane arrived and the pilot announced that he would be coming through there the next morning on his way to Fairbanks, and if there was anyone who needed a lift he would be prepared to take them. I immediately thought I should take the plane, giving me the chance to tell the bishop this had been a big mistake. Soon after the plane left, however, the whole valley was completely surrounded by storm clouds. Within a few hours the snow was falling so hard that life came to a standstill in the village; nothing was moving as the snow began to build up. There was no hope of getting to Fairbanks the next day. I returned to my mission house with no hope of getting out of this prison. I had wondered why I should get out of bed in the mornings since there was nothing to get up for except Sunday mornings. As the snowstorm continued over the next three days, I stopped getting up. I didn't eat. I slept. And then I became aware that I was being visited by practically everyone in the village. All ages came to see me. Young children brought me cookies. An elder came and sat with me. A couple, Henry and Jenny Smoke, along with their children, came to comfort me a number of times. When I look back on those three days, it was like the villagers had all gathered together to plan when they would visit me. They came along, in groups and alone, morning, afternoon, and evening, while the snow poured down outside.

"On the third day I awakened, probably about 9:30 in the morning, and the mission house was filled with bright light from outside. I climbed out of bed and pulled back the curtains and looked out on the most pleasant scene I have ever witnessed. The ground was covered with many feet of pure, fresh, white snow that had not been disturbed by wind, animals, or human beings. No one was about. The sky was ink blue. I have never seen the sky so deep blue as it was that morning. Quickly I got up and went outside."

Al looked at me, shyly, and said, "For me there had been no hope out of this predicament and now three days later it was Easter for me. This was my resurrection experience, and it was the people of Steven's Village who had ministered to me, who knew about me, more than I could ever imagine."

He said then that life didn't take a "grand 180-degree turn" but he did go trapping and hunting with the men from the village, he conducted Bible classes, and in May, when the ice broke on the river, he and the men cut logs above the village and rafted them down to build a new church. They dried the logs on the river's beach over the summer, and in the fall, before the snows, they used a Jeep to pull them to the building site. Two weeks later the building was up, Al said, with an altar, a fifty-gallon drum stove, and pews from the old community building. It still stands, Al said, almost forty years later.

I looked at Al and he looked at me.

"Tell me about yourself," he said.

Everything I had planned to say went out the window.

"My brother died a year ago," I said and started to cry.

I preached for the first time at St. Columba's in Advent, the beginning of the church year. I had to preach at the 7:45 service and then again at 10:00. I got up, having not slept much, grabbed my sermon and a box of crackers and headed for the door. Vincent rolled over in bed and said, "Break a leg." I drove south at over eighty, praying that all the cops were in bed or at some early morning service themselves, and tore into the parking lot where I recognized Al's little black Honda, like a little black clerical suit. I rushed in and met him coming out of the sacristy with a taper in his hand. "Here," he said, turning around. "Let's find you an alb that will fit."

Slowly the church filled with the early service crowd, mainly elderly people. We processed in, me in my alb with Al and Carri. I wasn't sure I liked marching up the aisle. I saw people looking at me, and recognized Marty and his mom. When we got to the altar area, and took our places, I looked back at the congregation and they seemed a very long way away.

The Gospel was John the Baptist crying in the wilderness.

"In this Advent season, let us all name our wilderness," I said, thinking of my own dislocation and grief at leaving Trinity, and of Al and his story: "Where must we go, where is the place we are called that has no maps, and different guides."

3

I'd been at the ministry study year for about three months, working almost every weekend, traveling to Camarillo several times a week. I sort of liked it. Sort of. Several of the other students in the ministry-study-year program were having genuinely bad times: Ken wasn't getting along with his rector; Kate's congregation in Malibu came from so many different parts of LA that people rarely gathered there on any day except Sunday, so it was hard for her to fulfill parts of her "contract"; another's mentoring priest seemed to be constantly critical.

Al Smith was kind to me, supportive, attentive, clear. He seemed tired of his parish, tired and irritated by the same people making the same complaints, and the lack of pledges coming in. There were those in his parish who were tired of him. But he was faithful. He became for me the definition of a faithful priest. He had been there for twenty-five years, and he still got up at five o'clock on Sunday morning and went to the church because he liked to be there when the sun came up. If the parish hall wasn't swept when he had a meeting there, he swept it.

One Saturday, he took me to see an elderly woman who lived in Leisure Village, row upon row of monopoly houses on streets so identical Al wouldn't let me drive there alone. She was in a wheelchair and breathed only with the aid of oxygen. It was a "pastoral visit," part of the work I had to do in this year of discernment. I had seen plenty of sick and elderly people in my years in the church and sat with my share of those who were dying, but those had all been friends. Here was a woman I hardly knew for whom I could do nothing. I felt awkward and unhelpful so I gave up and watched Al. He was calm and attentive, and, I realized, without charm. He did not rely on charm to get him through, but on something more muscular, learned maybe in the hard years in Alaska. He was there for her, sitting, a solid man, and I saw that she knew he would come back.

I felt ambivalent about the ministry study year. I liked the people at St. Columba's much more than I thought I would but I missed Trinity. St. Columba's was a good community, hard-won, but it was not an exciting place to me. Things I took for granted at Trinity were not in place here: inclusive language, experimental liturgies, cutting-edge justice work. The urgent questions of the day, which Trinity wasn't touching either, the grim condition of the environment, for example, or economic injustice, weren't even on the radar screen here. The diocese was cleverly showing me what the church was like, what a parish I might work in eventually would likely be. Few of them would be like Trinity. Fewer still, I suspected, would be as decent and as caring as Camarillo. The most I could hope for would be some place slow and steady, an island for the shipwrecked. Was this the work I wanted for my one life?

I was praying for a sudden bolt of lightning that would make everything clear when I happened to take a little time to hang out at my local bookstore. It had not been a good day. Vincent and I had had a near-fight late in the afternoon. We were talking about prayer in the schools. We were both against it, but in the discussion I began to inch toward talking about faith. I wanted to tell him what it was like to serve communion.

"I want some room, some leeway," I said. "I want a way to talk to you about this huge piece of my life."

"You have leeway," he replied. "I have always taken your faith seriously, but I can't always follow it. I don't believe what you believe."

I felt my chest tighten. "Let's quit," I said. "We aren't going to get anywhere." And so I went, with a heart of stone, to walk among books.

I was looking for a book by Frederick Buechner, called *Whistling in the Dark, a Doubter's Dictionary,* to give to a friend for Christmas. I couldn't find it on the crowded shelves, and there were so many people standing in the aisles that I finally went to the front desk to ask a clerk. She had a direct, clear gaze and long straight blond hair. Checking her computer screen, she said, "Yes, we have it." Then she looked at me and said, "It's in the Christian section." I had four distinct thoughts: She thinks I'm a fundamentalist. Then, She probably thinks I'm for prayer in the schools. Then, She thinks I'm a priest. Then, I am a priest. At that precise moment, I felt in the right place. I smiled at her. I had all the time in the world.

"Let me help you find it," she said, and we walked back to the shelves. She stood in front of the rows of books searching. Several women pushed past us, but we were like two rocks in a swift-moving river.

"It's not here," she said apologetically. "Maybe it's in the back room; we're reorganizing the shelves. But things back there are impossible to find."

I nodded. I felt as alert as a red fox I'd seen once high up on a cliff above a beach. I understood that it was important that I give my full attention to the clerk. Not the book, not thoughts about the rest of the day.

"I'll take your name," she said, "and if we find it, I'll call."

"Fine," I said, and we walked back to the front desk. I stood beside it. Several people pushed past me.

She wrote out my first name. "No 'h' at the end?"

"No 'h.' "

She spelled "Gallagher" correctly, putting in the "h" after the "g." This seemed to me an infinite kindness. I thanked her. She thanked me. We looked quizzically at each other for a second as if acknowledging that something funny had happened to us both and then I walked out. The calm and peace stayed with me for minutes. I kept trying to hold on to them, knowing they would fade.

I told Ann Jaqua.

"This is important," she said. "This also happened in the soup kitchen?"

"Yes."

"You said you felt she saw you as a priest?"

"Yes."

"As if she called it out of you."

"Precisely." I thought about it for a few minutes. "It happens sometimes in the church. It happened recently, but not the same way, when I was serving communion at the back of the church during the AIDS mass."

"It happens when you are serving," she said. "In the soup kitchen. At that communion. And, then, in a store?"

"Yes," I said. "I felt as if I were serving her, the clerk. But I don't get it. If anything, she was serving me. I was there for her, though. But why there?" And then I saw it, all of a piece. "Oh, it was a *book*store."

"Oh, of course," Ann said. "A bookstore."

I'd been at writing so long I didn't fully acknowledge it as a vocation on a par with priesthood, until that moment, and that it, of the two, had claimed me first. Sometime before I was twelve I knew I wanted to be a writer, but it was put into words that year. My parents went out to look at a ranch for sale west of Albuquerque, having had a fantasy for some time about living in the country. The owner was William Eastlake, the author of

Castle Keep, a novel about a group of American soldiers who hole up in a castle in Belgium during the Second World War. It was a hugely successful book, with rave reviews in *Life* and the *New York Times,* and would be made into a movie by Sydney Pollack staring Burt Lancaster. So there was glamour in the air. While Eastlake's wife served coffee, he asked me what I wanted to do with my life. I stood in front of him, as a child stands while an adult sits, and almost sniffed the air. I was aware of his glamour but also what felt like—I was not sure of this—disappointment. I realized then that one of the jobs of a writer was to see what was unseen or hidden, and then to have the confidence to find the words for it. I said, "I want to be a writer."

"Who do you read?" he asked.

"Hemingway," I said, in as tough a tone as I could muster.

"You might try Flannery O'Connor," he said quietly.

In my twenties, I worked as a journalist, and tried to learn how to write. It became the way I made sense of the world, but it was also a way of entering into the world. The world remains a mystery without a tool to enter it. One finds one's way in through falconry, or geology, or hunting ducks. Fishing or making baskets or boats. To this day, shop talk is among my favorite conversations, of any shop. What pens does a writer use, what notebooks. What weight of watercolor paper does a painter use. ("I once said to my students, 'My watercolor paper is so strong you can drive a truck over it,' " said a painter friend of mine. "So one day I decided to find out if this statement I had been making for years was true, and I drove my Jeep over the paper in the driveway.") Builders of Adirondack guide boats use the roots of spruce trees for the ribs; reporters get those thin brown notebooks that fit into jacket pockets from Richmond, Virginia. I was no longer a cork bobbing in a sea of one thing following another without distinction or difference, but a person with a hook, with a method, taking the world into my hands, entering whole new landscapes. I knew how to do it right away. Not that I knew how to do it well, but I immediately got it, apprehended it. Its tools attracted me; I loved its forms and rules.

Over the years, writing has required sacrifice. In order to have time to write, I've never worked full time and therefore have never made anything like real money. I've passed up things that would take away from writing for any long length of time: graduate school, long vacations, breakfast out. I've driven many old cars.

I don't know what mornings are like outside my studio. Mornings for me are spent in various sweatpant, T-shirt, and scruffy fleece pullover combinations, complemented by aging Ugg boots, hair sticking out, morning breath, hunched over my computer rewriting sentences. After three or four thankless hours, I head for the kitchen and eat lunch standing up. (A friend once suggested we invent something called "writers' kibble.") The next day, I do this all over again. (I once ran over to my next-door neighbor's house in my writer's fatigues, which that morning comprised a tasteful combination of a smelly flannel bathrobe and slippers, to see if she had a copy of the *LA Times,* as my first book had just made the bestseller list. She was standing in her kitchen with a nice man who turned out to be her contractor. I muttered something in my writer's breath, they both stepped away just a whit, and she got very excited and said, "This is my neighbor and she is a writer and she is on the bestseller list," and he looked at me with grave disappointment as yet another fantasy [Santa Claus, the Easter Bunny, best-selling writers] bit the dust.)

On the rare occasions when I do go out in the morning, I am as excited to be in downtown Santa Barbara as I would be if I were suddenly transported to Bombay. Streets! People walking to work! Newly mown grass in the park, washed sidewalks, the smell of fresh coffee.

But I don't do this more than once or twice a year because if I were to ever get in the habit of going out to breakfast, or doing something else in the mornings, then I might . . .

I had a neighbor, Rosemary, a woman in her eighties who wore only blue, a bent-over woman with a face half paralyzed by stroke, who pushed a shopping cart from the local Ralph's to her house once a week, agonizingly slowly. One day, I asked her if I could help her carry her groceries and she replied, "If I slow down, I might just stop forever." I knew exactly what she meant.

If I slowed down at writing, I might just stop forever. I realized, the evening of the incident at the bookstore, that was what scared me the absolute most about the priesthood.

My friend Cynthia, also a writer, whose mother was Episcopalian and whose Jewish father was born in Mexico, called and asked, "Why do you even need a priest? If you can pray to God directly, why does anyone need a priest?"

"A lot of people have asked that question," I replied. "Some of them very persuasively. Quakers mainly."

"Skip the kidding," she said. "How come?"

"Because someone has to lead the community, in the end. Someone has to step up to the altar, and be more or less trained for it. Someone has to be a doctor, someone has to be a judge. Someone has to hear confessions. . . . 'The priest of the community must be clearly identifiable and responsible if that congregation is to be healthy and even to survive,' wrote Urban Holmes."

"If it's that simple," she replied, "why are you having so much trouble with it?"

While we were riding bikes on a path to the university, Marie Schoeff, an artist who had just joined Trinity, asked, "Why do you want to be a priest?"

"I want to be there," I said, "at the crucial places of people's lives—birth, marriage, death. I want to serve the Eucharist."

"So you want to be close to the people," she said, changing gears as she rode up a hill. "You want to have a close relationship."

"Yes," I replied. "That's exactly right."

"Then I wouldn't be a priest," she replied. "I haven't talked to Mark in about six months. He's too busy.

"I think it might be like other professions. Lawyers, for example," she continued. "They think it's going to take them closer to what they care about and instead it takes them farther away."

Ev Simson asked me out to lunch.

"Don't do it," Ev said. "It's ninety percent administrative services, arranging meetings. You have a real spiritual life, and a real spiritual gift. Train that."

Dane Goodman, Marie's husband, also an artist, called and asked me to speak about "passion" at a forum at church. "Not how you were called to the priesthood," he said, "but how you are called to write."

How I was called to write. No one had ever used those words for it. I wondered, then, about writing as a vocation. What is a vocation, anyway?

"Every single one of us has 'good work' to do in life," said Elizabeth O'Connor, a layperson, in her book *Cry Pain, Cry Hope.* "This good work not only accomplishes something needed in the world, but completes something in us."

Frederick Buechner said, "Neither the hair shirt nor the soft berth will do. The place where God calls you to is the place where your deep gladness and the world's deep hunger meet."

There is an element of sacrifice in it, not as we commonly understand it, that is, Oh, here I am denying myself. "Sacrifice is not giving up something to get something else you want more," said the Jungian author Robert Johnson. "Sacrifice is the art of drawing energy from one level and reinvesting it at another level. . . ."

Writing feels like a sacrifice in the oldest meaning of the word: it is an offering, the words are placed upon an altar. Ann Jaqua said to me one day, "When you write, the words become a sacrament."

I wondered, not for the first time but now with real intensity, about my ambivalence about the priesthood. I had answered Cynthia's questions too quickly. Why was I so ambivalent? Did it have something to do with a need to realize the meaning of writing as a "lay vocation?"

The church has been in the midst of a struggle to understand what ordained ministry and what lay ministry are for, probably, most of its life, but in the last fifty years, that struggle has intensified. When the church set out to revise the Book of Common Prayer beginning in the fifties, the motivation was not only to replace archaic language, but also to give to laypeople much more of a place in the liturgy. When the revision was published in 1979, some of what had been relegated only to priests— chalice bearing, for example—was given to laypeople. Baptism became the foundation of ministry, not ordination. Education For Ministry, a program for laypeople to study in parishes, designed by one of the Episcopal seminaries, grew in popularity, despite its four-year commitment.

At the same time, priests were still in positions of authority, and because their theological training was so much more extensive, they were seen not as one source among several but as the only source. There was a lot of confusion between being leaders and being all-knowing, between being responsible and being tyrannical, between someone who served the congregation and being the one served. The priesthood had become a "profession," like the law, or medicine, and was subject to the same corruption.

"The more we advocate the professional image . . . the greater the gap between our theology and our implied intentions in ministry," wrote Holmes. "Theology talks about salvation by grace through faith, and professionalism talks about salvation by works." Or to take it one step further, professionalizing corrupts a call because it changes it from being for the benefit of others to accruing benefits for the self.

"You begin with a simple need," said my friend Andra, who worked in the community-based medical care program, "and then it becomes a way to have power, to keep others out, and it ends up separating everyone, even the leaders themselves, from the vitality of the community.

"I've noticed in doctors that they begin to feel as if they have 'to know all' and that means they really have identified with the gods. No one can know that much. I'm wondering, too, if there's an inverse relation between grandiosity and need. If you begin to feel like a god—and priests must feel this way, too—let's say it doesn't really feed you. What if, in fact, it 'eats' you up? You then begin to feel more intense emotional need but you are less suitable for it, less able to give. This leads you to deprive others."

As she spoke, I remembered an incident at Anne Howard's house. She and I were working on planning for a retreat day when Mark Asman called. He spoke to Anne for a few minutes, then asked to speak to me. When we were finished, he said, "Ask Anne what I should wear to next week's ordinations."

"He should wear a surplice," she called out. "And a red stole."

"A surplice," I said, feeling left out, having no idea what a surplice was or why a stole should be red, and having been offered no explanation. It was code-speech and neither of them clued me in and I was too proud to ask. It was as if two officers had closed rank.

At a training for lay Eucharistic ministers at a nearby parish, a priest, a woman, let the laypeople know in no uncertain terms that they could not touch the tabernacle, the small container where the blessed sacrament is kept, with their (grubby) laypersons' hands. This kind of craziness goes on despite low pay, long hours, and less respect in general for the profession of priest. "The smaller the pit," Vincent said, "the meaner the rats."

"We want to live a holy life," said a friend of mine who is a priest in Southern California, "and what we end up with is a fucking profession."

"The problem also comes, I think, not just from those who are on top," Andra continued. "We are trained over many years to revere the king or the president or the analyst or the priest in a way that makes us natural followers, wanting to be led. Our own impetus to know, to strive toward, to lead is diminished by our need to have someone to follow. Just the title 'layperson' is a diminishment, because it implies something that you are not rather than something that you are. You are not a priest, you are not a doctor, you are not a lawyer, you are a layperson."

I remembered what it had been like at Trinity, before we hired Mark Asman and after the priest who preceded him had left. For a few months, laypeople ran Trinity. It was a lot of work, and many jobs went undone, but we felt vital and excited. We had to pay attention; we couldn't just go to sleep in the pews.

Now, at Trinity, laypeople were very much involved in the actual running of the parish, as heads of councils, as vestry members; our administrative roles were clear and vital and pushed the envelope. But our theological and liturgical functions were fairly traditional: on Sunday, we served as acolytes, scripture readers, and intercessors, not as presiders or preachers. The education, training, and ordination of priests kept certain functions separate. And while there were good reasons for this, in the way there are good reasons to send a lawyer rather than a paralegal into a difficult criminal court case, were there *always* good reasons? And had they been thought through or just accepted?

How did what laypeople apprehended—in their daily struggle with faith and hope and despair and morality, in the family, in the workplace, in "volunteer work"—how did that flow back into the church community? How was it recognized? Trained? Used? And what about discernment? Didn't we all need, at different times in our lives, exactly the kind of attention I was getting: our peers listening for the song of the Holy Spirit on our behalf? How this worked itself out, I began to think, would determine nothing less than the character of the church in the next decades.

Was I the person in whom the struggle was embodied?

I did not wish to leave writing, I knew that, and now I realized it might be a real mistake to give up being a layperson.

Shortly afterward, I went up to the monastery to hear a series of lectures by William Countryman, New Testament scholar at the Church Divinity School of the Pacific in Berkeley, California, and author of *Living on the Border of the Holy: Renewing the Priesthood of All*. Countryman's title for his workshop at Mt. Calvary was "If You're Human, You're a Priest."

Countryman said that we are all part of a fundamental human priesthood. By "priest," he said, "I mean any person who lives in the dangerous, exhilarating, life-giving borderlands of human existence where the everyday experience of life opens up to reveal glimpses of the Holy. And not only lives there, but comes to the aid of others who live there."

He said he thought that "priestly interaction was characteristic of human life altogether." His definition of priestly interaction was in two parts: standing alongside another while he or she is encountering the holy and revealing secrets, or arcana, to one another. Countryman made it clear that he was not referring to the kind of secrets kept by the CIA or the type of secret we like to know about because it makes us feel powerful. (Or the sort of secrets that Anne and Mark used to close me out.) Arcana are secret because "they cannot not be; because there is no simple way to understand the world." Each of us has a special knowledge of life because each of us is "standing in a spot no one else occupies." Each of us has a unique perspective on the world, born of our own vision and experience, Countryman said. It is from this perspective that each one of us can reveal to another person our own arcana, our secret knowledge, about life's mystery or meaning. We absolutely depend on this in one another, because no one of us can know enough. Or, put another way, we are built to be dependent on each other to piece together how to live. No one person is supposed to have all the goods. We are built to be dependent on each other to be whole.

Countryman emphasized that he did not want to rid the church of ordained priests. Some people are called to what he called a "sacramental priesthood." But he would like the church to move away from definitions of clergy and laity that treat them as simple opposites of one another. "The alternative to the opposition between laity and clergy is not abolition of one or the other group or radical subordination of the one to the other, but a redefinition of both that acknowledges their interconnectedness. We need to move away from seeing the sacramental priesthood as standing "over and against the laity" and understand it as existing "in and for the fundamental priesthood."

The idea that we were all in this together, piecing together how to live, and that we all shared in a common "priesthood" pricked up my ears. A fundamental human priesthood would be a priesthood we were all called to incarnate, we were all called to live out. It sounded enormously demanding. It suggested a disciplined attentiveness to daily life, to opportunities for priesthood in the church, at home, and at work. It asked us to honor and sanctify both our own experiences in the borderlands, and those of others. A priesthood belonging to each one of us urged us all to discern ordinary events of life from those that represented "a call." It required teaching, listening, probably scholarship, and practice. It both demanded more of and elevated the role of laypersons in the church.

The idea of this fundamental priesthood harkened back to the church's past. For who were those women who presided in the house churches if they were not priests? And who were their companions? They were priests together, trying to live out this amazing story told to them by the men and women who were friends to Jesus. They were encountering the holy together, helping each other discover their true lives, celebrating at the tables in their homes.

We are built to be—I put myself back in those early house churches—a company of friends.

One night at the base community we had ended up talking about our daily lives in a particularly edgy way. David Reese, the lawyer on the vestry, told a story about a client. This client's partner had recently died. Her nurse called David one day and said she thought his client was committing slow suicide and wanted to talk to him. "I basically spend my days closing deals," David said, "and she wanted to talk to me. And I didn't know what to do."

"It is not as if God could not take care of her," he continued. "But there's this part we have to do, that I was supposed to do. I don't quite know how to put a face on it." I looked over at him. I could see him struggling to make sense of his life, as I was struggling to make sense of mine. He was struggling to make sense of what seemed to me to be a part of his ministry as a lawyer, something apart from "closing deals." And that we, as his base community, were meant to help him do it. In this little shabby church library, we were piecing together how to live. And then I thought, perhaps God doesn't know all the parts either but cranes her neck toward us, listening.

Just after Christmas, on "vacation" from St. Columba's, I preached on Simone Weil at the Thursday Eucharist at Trinity. I talked about how her life was influenced and organized by the politics and horrors of the last century: Marxism and the rights of workers, the Spanish Civil War, and, finally, World War II, Nazism, and the Holocaust. There was about her an excessive and sometimes outrageous purity that would not allow her to compromise. About Weil Robert Coles said it was important to find "where she was saner than some, and when she was probably a little loony."

In 1938, she had an experience that "marked her forever." During Holy Week at the monastery at Solesmes, France, in a dark chapel, suffering from a series of migraines, she began to recite George Herbert's poem "Love," trying to identify the pain she was feeling with the passion of Christ. At that moment, she felt "Christ himself came down and took possession of me."

Despite this overwhelming knowledge of Christ, Weil resisted baptism. She could not bring herself to "cross the threshold of the church" because she said she could not separate herself from "the immense and unfortunate multitude of unbelievers." (She was also repelled by the institutional church, its dangerous alignment with power, and its capacity to betray.)

How well I understand her, I preached. I stand here, I said, ambivalent about the priesthood, unsure of whether my vocation is finally to be a priest "inside" the church or, somehow, remain "outside"; "I am unable to cross the threshold."

Afterward, Mark Asman said to me, "Your life exhibits all attributes of a call, but to what? I am afraid it will be distorted if you name it too quickly. You understand the idea of layperson so clearly that to seek ordination feels to me as if you are joining the palace guard just as the revolution is breaking out."

Lent came early in 1998 and as part of the season, I had agreed to lead a series on "spiritual tools" at St. Columba's, which included walks on the labyrinth. One Sunday morning, I spread the large canvas out in the parish hall. I had hoped to attract a crowd, but only a few people showed up. The day before, I'd laid out the labyrinth for the Altar Guild, most of whom were elderly women. Each woman had a story to tell about her walk that morning, and about pieces of her history. We heard about death, and children, and lives with what they hoped was God that spanned sixty to seventy years. Later, at lunch, one of the members of the guild told me that during World War II, she didn't get a job as a secretary, but instead chose to work as a big crane operator in a munitions factory. I asked them at one point what it was like for them to serve on the Altar Guild. One of them laughed. "I've been serving for twenty years," she said, "and no one has ever asked me that question."

Another raised her hand. "It's something I look forward to," she said. "I don't know why."

"Why do you think?" I asked.

"Oh, it's something about the silence in the morning," she said. "I like to take the linens out and to feel them in my hands. And when I take them home—" She stopped.

"And when you take them home?" I asked.

"Well, this is kind of embarrassing, but I say a little prayer over the washing machine."

"What do you say in your prayer?" asked a woman with thin arms and a knee brace.

"Oh, I don't know," the first woman said. "Something like that it will all come out okay, that the stains will come out and the linens will get through the wash, and then that—" She quieted. "That all of us will get through, too."

No one said anything for a second or two and then a woman in her eighties said, "I cried when I walked that thing," pointing to the labyrinth. "I don't know why. I am embarrassed that I cried."

"Why?" I said.

"Oh, honey," she said. "You are not supposed to cry in church. Even though we are not in church, I mean in the actual building, we are still, you know, in a church setting. You are supposed to be upright and purposeful."

Said another, "I am not sure that is true."

The woman replied, "I am not sure anymore either."

On Sunday, a man I hadn't seen before showed up, a guy with graying hair, dressed in a blue sweater. He said his name was Carlos; he was a pediatrician, new to the area.

I asked everyone why they thought it was a tradition to remove one's shoes on holy ground, as we always walked the labyrinth in stocking feet or barefoot. No one said anything and the silence started getting awkward and then Carlos said, "Because you are more vulnerable without your shoes." Then more people spoke up. "You feel more in touch with the ground without your shoes." "You feel more humble." Then the ten or so people walked the labyrinth, including Carlos. Later, he came over to me and said that his uncle had died on Saturday, and that when he walked the labyrinth he "saw" his uncle's face in the window. "Thank you, for this," he said. "I needed this today."

Our ministry-study-year group met in a Sunday school room at All Saints Church, Pasadena. The walls had on them children's drawings of clouds. Nancy Larkin had come to speak to our group about what to expect in the year ahead. She arrived and began reeling off dates. When we would take the Minnesota

Multiphasic test. The appointment with a therapist who read the test. A criminal check. An appointment with the bishop. When she spoke of the appointment with the therapist, she said, "Just be careful to dress appropriately."

I looked over at Kay. I had known her long enough now to recognize that look on her face.

"Appropriately," she said quietly in a perfect Nazi accent. "Do you mean not to wear ze leather collar?"

"No," I said, matching my Nazi to hers. "Not ze one mit ze spikes."

Nancy looked momentarily nonplussed.

"Ha, ha," she replied. "That's right, Kay." And returned to her papers. Someone asked her if she had the dates written down and she said, No, she didn't, and Ann Jaqua offered to write them down and copy them for us. We took a coffee break while Ann found a copy machine.

Nancy walked over to me and asked to speak to me. I thought perhaps I had gone a little too far.

"I wanted to let you know about something that came up at the Commission on Ministry retreat," she said. I stopped stirring my tea. "It's about the fact that you don't have a B.A.," Nancy continued, while Ken brushed past us to reach the sugar.

"Yes?"

"Well," Nancy said, as Kay, laughing, walked past and then, seeing my face, stopped and arched her eyebrows in a question. I waved and mouthed, Later.

"Well," Nancy said. "It's about the problem of seminary. Someone, I can't say who, raised the issue of the problem of the seminary degree."

"Could we talk about this in a place a bit more private?" I said.

"Oh," said Nancy. "Of course."

We walked out into the large hallway, and sat down on a little colored bench.

"You see, you can't get an M.Div. if you don't have a B.A.,"
Nancy said. "And in this diocese at least that's a problem."

"But you can get an M.Div.," I said, my voice starting to rise.
"I told you about that before the study year began. At least two
seminaries will award an M.Div. without a B.A. if the student
does well. And all of the seminaries I checked on will admit me,
without a B.A., as long as I fulfill their requirements."

"Could you send me that information again?" Nancy said.
"I'll look into it."

"Yes," I replied. And we returned to the group.

Nancy left soon thereafter and David Duncan began his
lecture.

"How are we 'to sing our songs of exile in the promised
land'?" David began. "How can the church or yourselves express
faith, uphold virtue, be islands of love in a sea of violence? How
do we do this in a language that has integrity? Even our best
efforts are inadequate because we are fallible," he said, taking off
his glasses and looking out at us. "That's where the sacraments
come in—because we are fallible, I think."

When the morning was over, we broke for lunch. Tacos, prepared by one of the ministry-study-year students, a woman
lawyer. After lunch, I asked to speak to David and Ann and told
them what Nancy had said to me.

"Why did Nancy bring it up here, like that?" Ann asked.
"And who do you think brought it up? Nora talked at length in
her application about not having a B.A. Why is someone bringing it up now?"

"I don't know," David replied. "I'll do what I can to find out
about it, but I don't know that I will be able to. Try not to
worry."

"I think I'd better send all of the material from the seminaries again," I said.

"Yes," David said. "Send it all again. You might want to send supporting letters from the deans of admission you talked to before. Just to support your case."

As I drove home, I was furious. Someone had raised a serious issue regarding my application and this had been communicated to me during a coffee break in a ministry-study-year class. I was not to know who had raised the question. I had covered the whole ground in my original application and had been ready to answer questions regarding it during the first round of interviews. It certainly would have been much more appropriate to raise the issue at the interview stage, when I could have answered directly for myself. Maybe it's someone who didn't interview me, I thought. But the person could have asked the people who did.

And why did I have to do all the research on seminaries, once again? This was something the diocese should know, and have on hand, for candidates such as myself.

I spent the next several days contacting seminaries, forwarding their replies to Nancy, and worrying. The dean of the seminary in Berkeley spelled out why her college accepted a few students without bachelor's degrees: "The Association of Theological Schools (ATS) allows schools to admit up to 10 percent of their student body without baccalaureate degrees." She pointed out that there were students who do not hold a baccalaureate degree but clearly had the ability for graduate work as well as "gifts for ministry." She gave examples: a woman with a B.S. in nursing from a three-year school, a man with experience in business with the equivalent of an A.A. degree. "In our admissions process we wish to provide an opportunity for those without a degree to demonstrate their ability to do graduate work. Not to do so would deny the church some talented and committed leaders."

I called Anthony Guillén, who himself had not had a B.A. when he applied to seminary, and told him of the situation and asked his advice. He had not attended the commission's retreat and had not heard about the question raised about my lack of a degree.

On Sunday morning, I got up early and drove over to Trinity to meet Timothy Jolley, the monk from Mt. Calvary. He was driving with me down to St. Columba's to present part of the Lenten series I'd organized. Timothy's topic was *lectio divina,* the art of holy reading, a centuries-old practice of reading and rereading scripture and listening for the words that resonate. He had taught widely in the church, including several trips to South Africa, where he had conducted schools of prayer in the Benedictine tradition.

When I pulled into the small church parking lot, Timothy was standing next to the monks' corporate car, a small white Honda. He was dressed in his white habit and wearing Birkenstocks. He looked quite happy. He stuffed himself into my car, and I pulled out. I started to ask him how he was doing and he looked at me carefully, and said, "Well, this morning I got up very early because I hadn't figured out what I was going to say today, and I saw an owl. How are you doing?"

I started to tell him about the whole B.A. problem, and then I started to cry.

"Oh, Lord," he said. "Doesn't that sound like the church. I swear they put people through boot camp to get to be priests and then they are surprised when they turn out to share some traits with drill sergeants. Tell me how it's going at St. Columba's."

I told him of the walk on the labyrinth, and the altar guild and Carlos. "What's important is the old folks and the pediatrician," Timothy said firmly, as if he were reading a lab test. "Pay attention to that. This other thing, with the diocese, is just a skirmish." We had arrived at St. Columba's and he pulled himself out of the car.

"Scripture is our story," Timothy said to the small gathering. "It describes our connection with each other and with God.

Other traditions—Native Americans, Africans, Celts—use their 'lore' as a way of defining who they are. The stories for them are alive. We modern Western Christians relegate our stories to 'history' and don't really believe that they are the blood that flows through us." He pulled out of his pocket a sheet of paper. "I want to read to you from a prophet few of us have heard of, Habakkuk. I'm going to read it three times with a little bit of time between each reading. I want you to listen for the words that have meaning for you today." Timothy began to read, and when he was a few seconds in, I heard the words: "Although the fig tree does not blossom, the vines bear no fruit, the olive crop fails, the orchards yield no food." Or you lack a B.A. and someone's out to get you, I thought.

At the forum, a man raised his hand and said, "I haven't been in a church in forty years."

Timothy replied, "Well, as they say in other recovery programs, Welcome."

I asked Timothy on the way home if he would consider being my spiritual director.

"Of course," he said. "It would be a good way for me to pray more regularly." He handed me the Habakkuk piece.

"Read this in the morning and in the evening," Timothy said. "Let's talk in a few days."

As we parked at Trinity he said, "You know. You may or may not be called to be a priest but the whole thing," he continued as he lifted himself out of the car, "is for your salvation."

It became my Lenten discipline to get up in the morning and read Habakkuk and listen for the parts of it that resonated that day. One morning it was, "the fold is bereft of its flock." And the next it was, "and there are no cattle in the stalls." I saw the author, this man who had lived centuries before me, describing loss: those wooly sheep, the robust cattle. The whole thing was a litany of loss—orchards, vines, olive crops, fig trees, sheep, cattle. All the sources of income and status. Gone. So, day after day, I contemplated loss. What I saw, finally, during Holy Week, was that it wasn't loss I was worried about—I had not after all lost my job (my cattle, my sheep, my vineyards), and had not lost my status as a ministry-study-year student, not yet. I had lost my idealism and my naïveté. The church was, after all, an institution like others, with its own agenda. It was not a person, as the superior of the Immaculate Heart Community had pointed out. It was a place in which I could not only get hurt but hurt by a distant, cold hand. That was the danger of institutions: that someone could hide from direct confrontation, doing damage from far away.

And I felt helpless. Apart from sending in the information I had already sent in, and drumming up support among people I knew, there was very little—in fact nothing—I could do. And I did not know if there was someone actually gunning for me or if someone had simply noticed something she had not noticed before. But I did know by now that the priesthood was a form of a club or a place with semi-restricted entry. Not all of its restrictions were unreasonable, but some were. "It begins with a simple need and becomes a way to have power, to keep others out," Andra had said. And one of the worst things that can happen to someone in the process of trying to enter a club is to have undue attention focused on them. There I was, as Good Friday loomed, out in the spotlight, quite without protection.

Maybe I should just quit now, I thought, before they humiliate me. I'm not ready for the institutional church.

"Don't quit," Vincent said. "This is not the way to go out." I thanked him, in some surprise, and he smiled.

On Maundy Thursday, the commemoration of the Last Supper, I drove down to Camarillo, alone, missing my own home church during this solemn day of its communal life. It will be hokey down here, I thought; I want to be at Trinity. I sat in the pew, while going through the service, sinking deeper into silence and boredom. Then it came time for the stripping of the altar. Al and Carri stood up and began taking things away from the area—crosses, prayerbooks, anything near or on the altar. Then Carri walked over and removed the fair linen from the altar. Something in her movement caught my eye. She went away, and then returned with a basin of water and a cloth. Slowly, purposefully, she began to wash the stone. Her hands moved along its surface, stroking the contours, her body leaning into the task, her face solemn and exposed.

And I saw that Carri was washing the altar exactly as one would prepare a body for burial, exactly as the women must have planned to wash Jesus, exactly, as I broke into tears, as Rande and I had washed Kit.

On Easter Sunday, Vincent and I were invited to the monastery for a feast. As we arrived, the monks were serving cheese and wine in the long gallery. Various church folk were there, exchanging the traditional greeting on Easter. "The Lord is risen," said Allan to Ev Simson. "The Lord is risen indeed," Ev replied. Then Allan turned to Vincent and me. "The Lord is risen," he said to me and handed me a glass of chilled Chardonnay. "The Lord is risen indeed," I said and kissed him. Then Allan turned to Vincent, who looked at his feet. "The Lord is risen," Allan said. And then he paused. "Or so they say," he said, grinning, and Vincent laughed.

I visited the monastery often to talk to Timothy in the weeks following Eastertide, those weeks following the resurrection. I went to the noonday Eucharist and to vespers and listened as the monks prayed for an end to the death penalty and for the inmates Allan visited in prison and for peace in the Middle East. Sometimes the prayers seemed foolish to me, naïve in the face of so much. We prayed for an end to sin and violence and suffering. Yeah, sure, I would think. But at other times, those same prayers felt like the witness of men courageous enough to be foolish and hopeful. They were trying, in that Eduardo Galeano phrase, *"abrigar esperanzas,"* to shelter hope.

And I saw that they too suffered, that one of them suffered from depression and was taking antidepressants, that several were recovering alcoholics, that old age was limiting another's ability to garden and hike. Yet they showed up and kept praying.

One afternoon, I told Vincent about visiting there, tentatively, recognizing it as another attempt to speak to him about faith, and he said softly, "I think they are men who do not expect their faith to end their own suffering."

I thought of the resurrection in those weeks as Jesus tunneling back from death. How much work it must have taken him. What a lot of love he must have felt for us to put himself to the task.

My Habakkuk ended his litany of loss with sweet surprising lines, "Yet I will exult in the Lord, and rejoice in the God of my deliverance," even as his stalls were empty and his fold bereft. "The Lord is my strength," he wrote, and then the final phrase, "who makes my feet nimble as a mountain goat's, and sets me to range the heights." I loved the image of the mountain goats, like the ones I'd seen high up in Glacier National Park. When hiking, we would hear a sharp *plink plink,* like the higher notes of piano keys, and look up to see white-bearded goats with little black feet on a ledge that looked inches wide, casually munching grass. I will be like them, I thought, in the midst of this B.A. fear and fiasco and struggle over vocation and marriage. I will find small passages just wide enough for my feet.

4

In July, the fog comes in every morning and flattens Santa Barbara into a dull pancake. The mountains disappear, the trees turn gray. All shadows vanish, all contrast fades in a bank of moist blankness. I got up, brushed my teeth, and read Habakkuk. One morning I drove up to the monastery, as much to get above the fog as to pray with the monks, and stood outside with Brother Nick watching the white blanket float beneath us like a huge inland sea. We were in the new garden next to the staked tomatoes. Nick said he'd been reading Genesis.

"Eating that apple may be about consciousness instead of sin," he said, bending down to inspect a green tomato. "It may be about desire for wisdom, that sensuous fruit. But the price of this consciousness, of self-knowledge, is that we also know, among other things, about death, and we are exiled from Eden." He looked out over the garden walls and down toward the bank of fog. It lifted enough to reveal sandstone rocks, and the red bark of a California madrone below us. Then he said, "But maybe Christ promises something else, a better place than Eden, but at the cost of suffering."

"What kind of place?" I asked.

"Your guess is as good as mine," he replied.

As I left the monastery that morning, I thought about this new Eden and where it might be found. I thought about how the path to it would be made by suffering. I recalled where I had walked these last three years. It had begun so suddenly in the hospital corridors in Albuquerque, where I stumbled along, alone and afraid, under intercom voices, while Kit was fed by drip IVs. Then he and I had that interlude bought with platinum chemotherapy and radiation. Kit, Rande, Vincent, and me in San Lorenzo Canyon shaded with cottonwoods and stacked with rock plates where the dogs, Here Boy and Rita, tiptoed on ledges like goats. The deep snow in Water Canyon and the scent of pinions and pines. These, the last places he and I walked together, now loved and longed for and as lost as Eden. Then the terminals at LAX, gliding on moving sidewalks and waxed surfaces toward the carpets of planes. Then I walked behind him as he pushed himself along the fence of his backyard. Then the path from the bathroom to the living room. A narrower and narrower field, a smaller and smaller landscape, one step after another, until there was only breathing and a breath took the place of a step.

I was still walking. Even if it were possible for Kit to catch up to me, or come back to me from where he was falling toward light, I still had to walk, and in walking I separated from him, leaving him in the past's landscapes, in the canyon's willows and the sunlit rock, in the river crossing. There was nothing, nothing I could do. Even if I had wished to try to freeze myself to stop time, the clock moved forward, the hours tolled; I could only join him in the past, in memory, or imagine some odd heavenly future, but not here, not now. This was not where he lived anymore. "The becoming, the possibility for the making of new memories, is gone," said my friend Harriet Barlow. "And the myriad holes that one flesh filled are left."

Yet the geography where Kit walked was still intact, the bosque, the ruins at Chaco, the thick river's edge. I found myself in the wake of his death loving those places as if they had almost become his flesh. Memory makes landscape sacramental.

Later in early July, I spent two weeks at Pt. Reyes, at the tip of Tamales Bay, with two other women in a small writers colony.

We were perched above an estuary that was also a cattle ranch: black and white cows flowed home in the evenings, red-shouldered hawks skimmed the air at eye level in front of my small writing studio. We were fed huge sweet spinach salads and wild salmon, cooked perfectly, with a glaze of hollandaise sauce.

After working in the mornings, I hiked in the Point Reyes National Seashore. One day I walked on a deserted beach and came upon the unmistakable "M" print of a mountain lion. Pelicans bobbed in the water, their throat tubs full of fish, while pirate gulls nipped in to steal from them before the pelicans swallowed. I lay on my back and watched an adolescent osprey flap his wings in his birth nest. One evening, the three of us took a picnic to Tamales Bay. Men and women rowed sculls lit by lanterns on the water. We skinny-dipped in the moon's path.

"If you know one landscape well, you will look at all other landscapes differently," says a character in Anne Michael's novel, *Fugitive Pieces.* "If you learn to love one place, sometimes you can also learn to love another."

All around me was a thing that exceeded me in intelligence, freedom, and purpose, the sharp calls of osprey, a hawk dropping a snake writhing in the air to his mate swirling beneath him, words written in the air, things that could not be pinned down.

In a book I found in the house was a list of local birds with a graph of their prevalence in the area over the last fifty years. Nearly every one of them was in decline, and a few were extinct.

The world in its wildness felt then as fragile and as mysterious as the dead. At the Bosque del Apache, the day Kit died, I had sensed him returning "into" the world. In Pt. Reyes, I realized that the natural world had become, had in some odd way taken Kit's place, as my measure of authenticity. The natural world was becoming my moral compass. As David Ehrenfeld wrote in his essay on George Orwell, "What was nature to George Orwell? Simply put, I believe it was his model, his example of certain qualities that he wanted to emulate and did emulate in his life and in the art that was his work. . . . The first of these qualities is honesty; the second I have to describe with four different but related words: reliability/continuity/durability/resilience; the third property of nature that was important to Orwell is its beauty and serenity."

Ann Jaqua said she was having trouble reciting the Nicene Creed because it did not make sense to her. "I believe in the Father, Son, and Holy Spirit," she said. "I don't know what that means anymore. I have been thinking about what I do 'believe in,' what I have faith in. I know this so far: I have faith in the world's ability to regenerate itself."

Over and over in these last years, the natural world had given me the solace I could not find anywhere else. And of course that world was being destroyed then and now as I write these words, in copper mines, in housing developments, in SUVs, in the dumping of nuclear waste. It is more than simple destruction—that is bad enough—it is an annihilation of a field of knowledge, a source of solace, a loss, finally, to the soul. We are deliberately shrinking the place where we all might find a second chance.

But even as I had these experiences and thought these thoughts, my life when I returned from Pt. Reyes veered off track. I had heard nothing from the diocese regarding my "situation," as Timothy and I had come to call it, and that anxiety undermined my days. I did not feel mindful. I didn't have the concentration of a mountain goat. On a Monday, Vincent and I had an appointment with our counselor. We had a big fight right in the middle of it. She, exasperated, said, "Oh, why don't you do that at home?"

Anne Howard and I met to work on a retreat we were going to teach at the monastery, "Martha Unplugged." Our idea was to teach the Mary and Martha story: Jesus comes to lunch at the two sisters' house and, while Martha works in the kitchen, Mary sits at his feet listening to him teach. Martha gets irritated, and asks Jesus to get Mary to help her, but Jesus rebukes her, saying that she has chosen to fret and worry while Mary has chosen the better way. We planned to talk about how we had all bought into being Martha, not only like Martha in the story but also that diva of the perfect household, Martha Stewart. But Anne and I were both tired and irritable—probably from playing Martha too much—and I left comparing my haircut, unfavorably, to Anne's. The next morning, I drove down to the Patagonia company offices, where I edit sections of the catalog, and met with the new head of the marketing department, who talked about how the catalog should have more bulleted copy because "people don't read." Then in an edit meeting, one of the writers said something about wanting to help me with an essay, and I heard her trying to horn in on my territory and I said, "I could squash you like a bug."

I could dimly see that I was unraveling, but the bad part of unraveling is that you don't see it clearly while it's happening. "My father's house is a mansion with many rooms," wrote a friend. "Room of fear, anxiety, need to survive—very constricted, intense place. That's one. Room of love, spaciousness, gratefulness, peace. That's another. I step back and forth between them." How I longed for that room of love, that new Eden, but how was I to get there? I did not do any of the things that might help: I didn't pray, I didn't hike in the mountains behind Santa Barbara, I didn't rest. Why is it, the thirteenth-century Sufi poet Rumi asked, that we have to be dragged kicking and screaming into Paradise?

On a Thursday afternoon in early July, I met Mark Asman at Trinity. I was to take the Minnesota Multiphasic test; he was to "monitor" me. We walked upstairs to a room the teenagers had been using and Mark handed me a folder and left. I opened it.

Inside were simple instructions. Basically the test was a series of statements that one must mark either Agree or Disagree. I shuffled through the papers and realized to my horror that there were three hundred statements. And then I began.

"I think nearly everyone would tell a lie to keep out of trouble." ____Agree ____Disagree

"Often I cross the street in order not to meet someone I see."

"The only interesting part of the newspapers is the comic strips."

And then, "Most of the time I wish I were dead."

As I moved through the test, I collected favorites.

"I am afraid of using a knife or anything very sharp or pointed."

"I hear strange things when I am alone."

"I feel uneasy indoors."

I realized, as I proceeded, that the test asked some of the same questions two or three times, in different places, and differently phrased—a clever mechanism to catch lies.

I was fairly sailing along—I don't really have any problems with knives—when I got to the coup de grace: "I have never engaged in any unusual sex practices."

Oh, no. I stopped, pencil poised in midair. My mind froze. What exactly was an, uh, unusual sex practice? This was why I hated the whole idea of these tests in the first place and had not wanted to take this one. Who wrote the test? What was his idea of sex? Did he, like me, grow up in the sixties? I doubted it.

Then I placed the pencil on the page and lied.

When I finished, I felt as if someone had been probing my psyche with a particularly blunt instrument. ("After completing a personality test, I feel like murdering its authors. Agree/Disagree.")

Then I felt anxious for a solid twenty-four hours.

.   .   .

At our regular ministry-study-year Saturday, we checked in. Ken complained that he wasn't getting along with his mentoring rector, that they didn't see eye to eye.

Kay reported that it was the summer in her parish and she had been leading a vacation Bible school with the kids.

None of our ministry-study-year parishes were growing, or at least not by much. (Some of the parishes we had come from were—ordinands often come from thriving parishes.) I couldn't shake the feeling that we were part of a chain of shrinking islands. The Episcopal churches that were growing in the United States were mainly conservative and in the deep South. Trinity, with its mixture of social justice and elegant liturgy, was probably an anomaly, although at least one author's study indicated that urban churches whose focus was on social justice were attracting Baby Boomers. As I listened to people report on their parishes, it all seemed increasingly out of touch, especially the language of the church: Vacation Bible School, Altar Guild, stewardship. When I spoke to friends using these words it was as if I were speaking Greek.

Yes, as a Baby Boomer I had to remember that while my generation was large and influential, there were many other generations in the church, many of whom were more faithful than mine. Not everything in the church should be changed to meet the needs of people my age. Yet I could not really judge a liturgy or a prayer except by what moved me, and hope that some of it had universal appeal. I was surprised to find that women in their eighties liked the labyrinth and that teenagers responded to my sermons.

Yet I wondered, once again, what I was doing here. I felt less and less sure of wanting to work as a parish priest, at least in parishes like Camarillo or the parishes I was hearing about in the ministry-study-year gatherings. They were caught up in planning Bible schools, the soon-to-come fall stewardship campaigns, the Christmas pageant, its own little world, a template created years ago. In the thirties, according to a priest-consultant, people went to church because they were afraid of not going to heaven; after the war, they went because it was a way to make friends; in the sixties, it became a vehicle for social change; and now in the late-twentieth and early twenty-first century, it was a place to find spiritual renewal and to meet others in small groups. Unfortunately, parishes included people from each generation, with each of these expectations, blended together in an uneasy mix. I, having grown up in the sixties, wanted the church to be more involved in social change and spiritual renewal. But St. Columba's was made up of people largely from older generations and young families; my concerns weren't theirs.

I felt more and more a fish out of water. I didn't fit easily into the role of institutional leader. I wanted to deepen my life. I wanted to anoint and be anointed, preach and listen, celebrate the Eucharist with the whole community participating because it is the community that makes the Eucharist, not a priest saying magic words over bread and wine. I still wanted to wear pretty robes. I wanted to "live" that "holy life," as my priest friend had said. I didn't want to spend half my time overseeing stewardship, running vestry meetings, and planning pageants. Was this naïve or prophetic?

As we were discerning, the church was discerning as well. The priesthood was changing, the role of the "laity" was changing. One of my classmates said discerning in the midst of so much change was like driving down a dark road at eighty miles an hour with no headlights.

When I got home from the Saturday session, the phone rang; it was Anthony Guillén.

"We met today about your B.A. situation," he said. (Everyone was referring to it as my "situation.") "We looked up precedents and it seemed appropriate to send the whole thing to the examining chaplains, a small group whose job it will be to evaluate your readiness for graduate work. So, that's the status. They will review your files and get back to us as a full commission. I think they will try to meet as quickly as possible."

"Is there anything more I can do?" I asked.

"No, I think they have everything they need," he said.

Through the grapevine, I heard that the chair of the committee was Victoria Hatch, the first woman ordained to the priesthood in this diocese, a woman with a keen mind and a matter-of-fact personality, who did not play politics or favorites. I felt a faint sense of hope.

On the day of our Martha Unplugged retreat, I dragged the labyrinth up to the monastery and pushed it into a corner. Women arrived pulling wheeled luggage and congregated in the monastery's main salon. They looked conservative—blow-dried hair, careful khaki pants—and I made one of my instant judgments about people I have never met: not interesting.

In the morning, Anne Howard taught a Bible study on Mary and Martha. Some of the women told stories about when they had been like Martha, resentful, plugging away in the kitchen, and when they had been like Mary, contemplative, worshipful. But then one of the women piped up, "I am getting angry at Jesus in this story. I mean, who does he think is going to make lunch!" And that broke the ice, and they began to talk more openly.

Then, in the afternoon, Melinda Menoni, a laywoman who was leading the retreat with Anne and me, pulled out a stack of white chef's aprons, as well as glue guns, buttons, colored pens, felt, old magazines, pipe cleaners, and glitter. She invited us to use the aprons as a canvas to tell a story either about when we had been like Mary or like Martha or to tell any part of our spiritual journey. We could glue onto the aprons pictures or photos we'd brought from home, or sew or draw on them. The women scattered around the large monastery room, cutting pictures out of magazines, firing up the glue guns, lips pinched in concentration. I have never been good at arts and crafts, nearly flunked home ec in eighth grade, had never touched a glue gun; I wanted to run from the room. But as I circled it, and watched the women, I began to slowly collect things that appealed to me: buttons, a gold pipe cleaner, a piece of yarn.

Several hours later, Melinda invited us to talk about what was on our aprons.

Some of the women told moving stories, but I was getting sleepy, and a little bored. My thoughts were of the chaplains' committee and my woes, and work undone—my cattle stalls empty, my flock dispersed—when a thin, quiet woman stood up and held up her apron. Her apron had a long thin green stripe on it, an aqua ribbon with a bow, and a photo of a young woman caught in its strands. She pointed to the long green stripe and said, "This is my depression." The room became still. Then she pointed to the photo and said: "And this is my daughter." Then, she pointed to the bottom of her apron, on which there were words written in Latin. She paused, and then went on. "This is the inscription over the door at The Oaks, a psychiatric hospital in Las Encinas.

"I go to the Oaks when I cannot stand it anymore," she said. "We call it the Schiz Ritz. I read the words over the door when I go in, each time, and they give me some kind of dignity." And then she paused and collected herself and said, "And it is where my daughter is now."

And then the woman read the inscription on the bottom of her apron. *"Non est vivere sed valerie vita,"* she read: "Not only to live, but to live valorously." And if we had been magi then, we would have gathered up our gifts and traveled toward her, toward someone who was not only willing to shape her vulnerability into words but brave enough to speak them.

Not only to live but to live valorously. I was wide awake now. She had given me a glimpse of that new Eden, an Eden in which we are invited to listen and to speak. To listen to a voice from someone or something not heard often in the old Eden, a woman suffering from depression, or the call of an osprey. The suffering voices within ourselves.

I thought of us then as a community of ears, pressed to the earth, to hear the gentle footfalls of the one who is always coming into the world. He offers in place of security the adventure of longing and the fragility of love. He offers a wholeness bought at the cost of suffering. We need to be ready to leap onto that tightrope or else that love will not come. I remembered that in Genesis, God invited Adam and Eve to name the created order, not to subdue it, because naming is our human gift. In this new Eden we would be invited to name the world again, to name it anew, to name and be named, to listen and to speak, to gather up our gifts and travel toward a new Eden bought at the cost of suffering, an Eden of others.

5

In late summer, the deacon who volunteered at St. Columba's went on vacation, and Carri was away as well. Al asked me to take Brent's place in the service. Deacons are not really subpriests although they are often treated that way. Deacons are meant to go out from the church to the poor or the marginal—originally they were sent out to bring the Eucharist and food and clothing to widows and orphans—and to bring back to the church news of those on the margins. They are supposed to remind the larger church of its duty to those who are silenced and powerless, and to bring to them the comforts of the church and the shelter of its influence and power. In the Sunday liturgy, deacons traditionally read the Gospel, prepare the altar for communion, and give the dismissal at the end of the service. To prepare the altar, you unfold the corporal, bring the serving chalice and paten from a side table to the main altar, open the prayer book and situate it so the priest can easily read from it, and receive the bread and wine when it is brought up from the people. Taking the deacon's role in the liturgy is not a complex job on the face of it but it's dicey because you have to step in and step out of the action throughout the service, so you can't go on automatic. Plus, you have to perform in front of the whole congregation the whole time. I met Brent a few days before he left on vacation at the church to practice moving in and out of the action in some semblance of grace. I would have to preach that morning as well, so I had a number of things to remember on very little sleep.

I got to the church late that Sunday, as usual, struggled into my alb, placed my sermon on the pulpit before too many people had arrived in the pews so that I wasn't messing around near the altar as they tried to pray, and then reminded myself what exactly a deacon was supposed to do. I should have had a cheat sheet. And there was, as it turned out, one more part I was to play, something deacons do, that I had not counted on.

I got through reading the Gospel and preached my sermon. Then, as the choir was singing the anthem, I stood up and walked over to the little table where the chalice and paten were kept, and made it to the altar without falling down or dropping something. I spread out the corporal on the altar, remembering to place the cross in the middle and the edges just so, and smoothed it out. I was reminded of setting a table before a dinner party, something I've liked to do since I was a child. I would have liked to have put in a few more touches—some napkin rings perhaps and a vase or two—but it was my first time. I received the elements from the ushers without mishap, and went back to my seat. Then, just as Al was chanting the *te deum,* one of the acolytes fainted. He was kneeling about twenty feet away from me, all the way on the other side of the altar, and one minute he was kneeling there and the next he pitched sideways. Al was in the middle of the prayer. I would like to say that I stood up and ran over to help him, but I didn't. I froze. In a matter of seconds, one of the lay Eucharistic Ministers grabbed him and a guy from the congregation got up and walked over to him and put a hand under his head and the kid came to.

Then it came time for communion. I stood, walked over to assist, expecting to receive a chalice, and Al handed me instead a paten full of bread. It came as a complete surprise. I hadn't realized that if Carri and Brent were missing, it left Al and me to serve bread. I carried the paten over to the altar rail where Sandra was kneeling, and she opened her palms. It was as if a bird had unfolded its wings right in front of me. I took a wafer and placed it in her hand. I said, "The body of Christ, the bread of heaven."

Then I moved to the next person. I waited until he readied himself, until he, too, opened his hands. Each person had to give permission. I thought of Kay. I wondered if this was what God was doing—waiting, patient, respectful—while we worked on how to get those hands to open. Serving the bread was much slower and less sloppy than serving the wine. I got to look into people's faces. I got to touch their palms. I thought about those men in prison with their empty hands and how they had given themselves to each other as the body of Christ. We are the body of Christ, I thought. We are the bread of heaven.

At the end of John's Gospel, there is a small resurrection appearance, hardly worth a mention against the others, no locked doors, no vanishing acts. Peter and his crew are out fishing—it's after Jesus has died and one imagines them sorrowful, empty. They've caught nothing. And then a man from shore yells out to them to cast their nets on the other side of the boat. Dubious—they've tried this—they try it again and catch so many fish their nets begin to break. Peter recognizes his Lord, jumps into the water, and swims to him. And when he gets there, Jesus is cooking fish on the beach. I thought of Jesus the Sunday I served the bread. I thought of him as the man who calls out to us from the shore, the man who cooks breakfast after a long night of work. After his death he is a more humble man; he doesn't heal, he has no dark fantasies of the end of the world, he does not proclaim himself either the son of man or much of anything else. The gist of what he says is mild and low: love one another, forgive each other, feed each other.

Faith is only an approximation, as is memory—one never knows if one has the real thing in one's grasp. It's always only a reaching toward, but that day when I served the bread I thought that I knew something of the man Jesus by handing out his body, that he was much lower than I had thought before, much sweeter. He was like the movement of a crane's wing, or a brother's habit of saying, "baby sister," or a woman suffering from clinical depression who is brave enough to want to live valor-ously. He was like all of these things, these movements, tied together, or he was the thing that tied them together. Maybe this was what was meant by communion, that he was still at it, help-ing us along, calling to us from shore. And we are meant to respond, to jump into the water, to swim toward him and toward each other.

On the day Harvey Milk and George Moscone were mur-dered by Dan White in San Francisco in 1978, I was reporting for *Time,* and I was sent out into the streets to gather "the people's response." I ended up at city hall, having rushed across the Bay Bridge from a class I was lecturing to in Berkeley. Crowds gath-ered there, the site of the murders, in a park across the street from the broad front steps. Thousands of people had come there, by instinct, to stand quietly, just stand, or talk softly. I was standing next to a woman wearing a luxurious mink coat. She was not really, I said to myself, my kind of person. Too rich, wearing fur. Then Joan Baez stood up on the steps of city hall with a micro-phone and started to sing "Amazing Grace." And we all started to sing with her. And I reached over without thinking and took the hand of the woman in the fur coat and she took my hand and we stood there, singing and holding hands with tears running down our faces.

At the end of his essay on faith, the English composer Syd-ney Carter writes: "Do I have this experience or do I just imag-ine it? Is it nothing but possibility, like a song that is asking to be written?

"If that is all it is, that is good enough for me. That, after all, is one kind of reality, perhaps the only kind of religious reality. Song, God, a waving possibility: you must trust it, travel with it— or it is not there."

This is good enough, I thought that day in front of city hall, holding the woman's hand in the crowd, and as I finished serv-ing communion at St. Columba's; this is good enough for me.

. . .

I had lunch with my discernment committee after church. We began by checking in about our lives.

Each one of them talked about pain they were suffering, in large and smaller ways. I felt as if I were abandoning them just as I was getting to know them.

Batie walked with me to my car.

I looked at her large hands as I got in, as if to photograph them.

I drove down to Los Angeles to meet with Dr. B., the therapist who had read my psyche tests. I had taken several more besides the Minnesota Multiphasic: a sentence completion test; a series of drawing tests (draw a person of the opposite sex, draw your family, draw a person in the rain—I never figured out what those were about). "Plan to take several hours with Dr. B.," Nancy Larkin had said. Dr. B.'s office was in a little run-down church in a little run-down neighborhood just north of LA proper. He greeted me at the door and led me into a small anteroom. He was small and nondescript and detached. He wore a pair of worn Hush Puppies and a pair of brown polyester pants that looked as if they were molting. He reported to me that I had "passed" all the tests. He said he was surprised I had not come out higher on the "altruism" score on one of them, and looked over his glasses for an explanation. I said something about how I was trying to take better care of myself these days by drawing boundaries, thinking, How in hell do you measure altruism? He said that on the vocation tests it was clear that ministry was appropriate for me. After we'd talked for an hour, he suggested I go around the corner for a sandwich. In the afternoon, we went over more of the tests, and talked about my family, Kit, how hard I worked. It was a perfectly strange conversation. I realized that the test process was only partially about finding out about candidates for priesthood; it was also about protecting the diocese from lawsuits. If a priest went off her rocker, the diocese could say they had done all they could to examine her before ordination. It left a bad taste in my mouth.

On the way home I stopped at a huge electronics store in Burbank I'd heard about, mainly just to see it, and also to check on the prices of computer software. Vincent and I were supposed to go out to dinner at 6:30 and I arrived on the dot. He was standing in the living room.

I kissed him and said, "Let me just change my shoes," and went into the bedroom. In a few minutes, I came out. He was silent. I chatted about the day, but got no response and then I said, irritated and somehow off balance, "Are you angry at me?"

He replied, "I am seeing a pattern of you making me wait." And then he was silent.

I waited for something specific. "When?" I finally said.

"Just now," he said.

"But we were supposed to meet at 6:30," I said.

"Yes," he said.

"It was 6:30 when I came home, and I was ready a few minutes later."

"You are not listening to what I am saying."

"I am listening," I said, irritated and defensive. "I disagree with you. I did not make you wait. I walked in the door at 6:30 and I changed my shoes."

"Okay, Ms. Counsel for the Defense," he said. "I can see you don't want to hear anything bad about yourself."

"No, that is not true," I said. "I disagree with you. I don't agree with what you're saying."

"No," he said and walked toward the door. "You just don't want to hear anything bad about yourself. I don't want to be with you right now." And he left.

I stood there. I couldn't move. I knew that this was about

something else but I didn't know what it was. Our counselor had been working with us on just this: on how we got hurt and what we did not say.

When we went to see her that week, we described the fight.

She asked me if I had been feeling defensive for coming in later than I had expected, whether or not I was actually "late."

I had to admit that I had.

"And did you?" she asked, carefully. "I am not saying that you are at fault. But did you then, by your tone or your manner, somehow, this is to put it much too bluntly, 'pick a fight'?"

I had to say that I did.

Then she turned to Vincent. She asked him if he had been feeling left out or "disrespected" in recent days. He said, Yes, he had.

"Her mind has been on church matters and this therapist appointment," he said. "I haven't felt much in the picture."

"And did you then, let her have it, in this exchange, without really telling her what you had been feeling?"

"Yes," he replied.

We were quiet, both of us, eating our own humble pie.

"So, how do we stop doing this?" I asked her.

She replied, "It will sound much more simple than it is to do. It is the thing we all have to do. You both have to take in, accept, admit to, more of your darker or more vulnerable sides. To put it simply: You both have to enlarge your capacity to suffer."

I dreamed I was an angel trying to break into being a human being. In the dream, I said to Ann Jaqua, "I'm not that scary; I'm only ten feet tall. And my wings aren't part of me, they're part of the universe."

· · ·

In the morning, I answered the phone and it was Anthony Guillén. He said, "I have good news."

"Tell me," I said.

"Victoria Hatch will be sending you an official letter, but the examining chaplains have decided that you are free to continue the ministry study year, what there is left of it, and that you may apply to those seminaries that allow it, without a bachelor's degree."

I thanked Anthony for all his help and he replied, "*De nada.* Godspeed."

I called Timothy, and he laughed.

"I'm glad to know there are some sensible people in the church," he said. "Now, I wonder, what will you decide?"

My year at St. Columba's was winding down. One of the last things I did was to arrange a labyrinth walk for the youth group on Sunday evening. I drove down with the labyrinth and laid it out in the parish hall. Carri was there and she and I laid out several large rolls of butcher paper on the floor of a smaller adjoining room for the kids to write on, if they wished, about their experience walking or as prayers. I asked them when they had gathered to tell me a bit about how they might imagine making sacred ground. One of them said, Turn out the lights, we'll light candles. Another said, Take off our shoes. Another said, No talking. To show respect, because you are closer to the ground. And so together we prepared the ground. We laid out votive candles in holders on the edges of the labyrinth, we turned off the lights, we took off our shoes. Thirty-five kids, ranging in age from twelve to eighteen, Carri, me, and a couple of parents who were helping to supervise. I stood beside the entrance to the labyrinth, and touched each kid on the shoulder to let him or her know that it was time to go in. I had decided to do this to keep the labyrinth from becoming too crowded, but it became a way of knowing them, of standing with them, a kind of intimacy.

"How will I make all the decisions I have to make in my life?" wrote one of the kids on the butcher paper. And "Will my cat make it for another year?"

They were quiet for a group of kids. After they walked, they tended to go out to the butcher paper and write for awhile and then come back, and sit, on the corners, near the votive candles. Soon there were little heaps of kids on all the edges and a larger pile in the middle. One of the mothers decided to walk and in the midst of it, I noticed she was looking as if she were holding back tears. Her daughter, also on the labyrinth, put her hand on her shoulder and whispered, "Why don't you just cry, Mom?"

I thought, Jesus loves us because he fell in love with us, with our sorrows and our struggles and our attempts not only to live but to live valorously. In the same way I had fallen in love with them.

6

At Chaco Canyon, the doorways have stone benches built into their sides, so a person could sit and rest, or wait, before passing through to another room. The doors line up. In one of the big houses, you can look through one door and see another and then another, one by one, down the long line of sight.

"I am haunted by the strangeness of the universe, by its sacredness as well as by its obviousness," said Richard Holloway, retired Anglican bishop of Scotland. "From time to time I have crossed invisible thresholds into other dimensions of reality. Another way to put this is to say that I believe in God. I find myself encountered by a depth in life that religions call the sacred or the transcendent. I also believe that Jesus of Nazareth was possessed by that mystery with a force that still reverberates today."

I preached my last sermon at St. Columba's in mid-October. The Gospel was from Luke, a story about ten lepers who approach Jesus, begging to be healed. He talks to them and then sends them away and as they go they realize they are "clean." Only one, a Samaritan, returns to thank Jesus. Jesus is dismayed that none of the others have come back—"only this foreigner"—and Jesus says to him, "Your faith has made you well."

He never says, "Aren't I something?" Or "Bow down before me because I did this for you." He says, "You did this. It was your faith."

I looked out on the congregation: the gray heads of the

women from the Altar Guild, the food ministry folks; Judy, Batie, David, and Bill; the youth group. I glanced over at Al and Carri and Brent. At Marty. I was struck by their sacredness and by their obviousness. And how their faith brought them back here, again and again. Finally, I said, "We are all here together, all of us pilgrims seeking our true home. You have made a home for this pilgrim this year at St. Columba's. When I think of you, I think of a prayer written by a nun in Ireland: For what was, thanks. For what is to come, yes."

I returned to Trinity like someone who had been in exile. I did not feel that I was the same person as the one who had left a year before. I was no longer "a layperson," but something between laity and priest, a hybrid, a crossbreed. It is typical of exile that it changes you, and when you return, you don't fit in the way you did before. I could not figure out what my role would be: what was I to do, join the stewardship committee?

But I was pushed immediately back into Trinity as if Trinity were reminding me of its life in me.

Elizabeth Corrigan had taken ill earlier in the fall. The various ailments that had plagued her over the last years—recurrent infections, colds, a bad back—combined to bring her down. She was moved from the apartment she lived in at the retirement home to two rooms there, with round-the-clock nursing care. I sat with her one day as her friend Basil Meeking, the Roman Catholic bishop of Christchurch, New Zealand, was packing to leave after a visit. He changed into his clericals, as Roman Catholic priests do when they travel, like soldiers traveling in uniform. Mark Asman dropped by and the two of them embraced at the door.

"Isn't it lovely," Elizabeth said to me, "to see two people who love each other saying good-bye?"

She was now wheelchair-bound and I picked her up for the

Thursday-night service each week for a while. One evening, when we were leaving the service, Mark rolled her chair out to my car.

"Okay, Elizabeth," he said, "put your arms around my neck and I will lift you into the car." He maneuvered her out of her chair and into the seat beside me, his arms firmly placed on her back, their hips pressed together. Before she released her arms from his neck, she grinned wickedly up at him and said, "This is a lot like making love, isn't it?"

"Why, yes, Elizabeth," he replied, clearing his throat. "It is indeed."

Then she could not get out of bed without assistance nor make her way to the dining room, and so she was moved again, this time to one room in a nearby convalescent hospital. Her huge life—which had begun as an orphan girl; moved into a sexy, big marriage to a renegade bishop; four sons; friendships with Dorothy Day and Daniel Berrigan—was now coming down, as grain or flour or water narrows into the throat of a funnel, to this. Dan Corrigan had said near the end of his life, "When you get old, it's like going down into a dark hole but at the end is a new light which you have not seen before and would not otherwise have had."

Ann Jaqua and Mark Benson and I visited her and we stood around her bed sipping clandestine sherry. When the rest left, she called me over. "You are a priest," she said quietly and firmly.

One day she breathed, but did not wake up. Her family gathered, and day by day we sat with them in her room, among the photographs and few remaining books. And then Ann Jaqua called on Monday morning, November 9.

"Elizabeth died this morning at 2:00 a.m.," she said, and I sat down on the floor. She was ninety-six.

. . .

Almost a week after Elizabeth's death, on Saturday morning, I drove down to Los Angeles for the second round of interviews with the Commission on Ministry. I was less nervous this time, but more frightened. I was no longer afraid of the members of the commission, but of "the call" itself. Timothy urged me to be as clear as I could be about its shape and nature and then see how it matched up to what was available in the world, not the reverse.

As I drove south, I thought about all the ways I had sought to elaborate and understand, to discern in community my own inchoate yearnings toward a "priestly" role. I was a layperson drawn to the sacraments and to a vision of lay ministry. I felt strongly that the ministry of laypeople had been neglected in the church. Even if I became a priest, that would be my focus. "A prophetic priesthood," my Trinity discernment committee had said. "A priesthood that recognizes and helps to call out of people gifts of lay ministry and at the same time calls out of the church the shape of things to come."

I did not wish to leave the ranks of the laity, as Simone Weil refused to leave "the immense and unfortunate multitude of unbelievers." Some part of me felt that if I became a priest, I would betray them, us. I thought of a woman who served on the vestry at a church in Thousand Oaks, south of Santa Barbara, and what she had said about lay ministry. Holly said she'd thought about how priests wear collars. Collars denote vocation, authority, she said, a sign of God's presence to the world. And they also provide a kind of protection. When a priest puts on his or her collar, he or she puts on a way of being, and a shield.

Laypeople don't have such protection, Holly said. Then she added, "We actually wear invisible collars." She said she'd been imagining herself, at different times throughout the day, wearing an invisible collar. "And it changed me," she said. "My entire perspective changed, from one of habitual self-absorption to an acute awareness of 'the other.' I forgot about me and was only concerned with those around me."

If I was ordained, I might lose track of the needs of laypeople, because needs arise from experience. I'd been happy preaching at St. Columba's but not so happy at the altar, dressed in an alb, separated from the congregation by twenty feet of tiled floor. Separation from laypeople was key to the priesthood, at least as it was presently practiced. Separate retreats for clergy, separate meetings with the bishop, separate seminars, separate places from which to worship. Separate chairs, separate clothing, separate lives. All that I had been initially attracted to, now felt like a dangerous disunity.

And I still didn't like the professional club aspect of priesthood. As a writer I had guarded my marginality, knowing that with the margins come freedom and perspective. The freedom to see what others are afraid to see, the freedom to write what others have a stake in not admitting.

It felt wild, this "call," this prompting; it seemed to share in the wild nature of the birds at the Bosque del Apache in New Mexico, and of the hawk that had passed over the hood of my car. The sacraments, because they were finally inexplicable, were its calling card. I feared domesticating it. It did not easily match up with what I had seen of the professional priesthood.

Yet I ached when I imagined not being able to serve the bread or to preach, except on rare occasions. I would not find out what it was like to preside at the altar, officiate at a wedding or at a funeral, or anoint someone in the hospital. To continue life as a layperson felt, now, to be incomplete.

I pulled up at the gates of the diocese parking lot, feeling more like an old hand, spoke my name into the little black microphone, and the gate opened.

In the first interview, the new chair of the commission, a

laywoman, Mari Mitchel, sat at the head of the table, with a gentle-looking man who introduced himself as Mark Weitzel, a priest working in a parish in Glendale.

I asked him what it had been like for him to work as a priest.

"Often very rough," he said. "How I experience vocation and priesthood is that it's not necessarily the thing I'm best suited for, but it is the only thing that feels natural. I might well be better at other things; I just can't, at least not now, do them. So there's a strange tension and it can lead to feelings of insecurity.

"And though, as a priest I'm surrounded by people, involved in their intimate lives, priesthood is intensely lonely, because I'm called to be priest and spiritual friend, not their pal. If I were functioning as a pal, I would not be able to be what I think God wants me to be with them. It's up to me to define that relationship and it's a formal relationship. You don't have normal friendships in the parish, nor should you.

"The paradox is, the reason I'm in it, is that I see community working, and there's nothing more beautiful. That is a place where there is no loneliness."

He paused and then went on, "One of the ways of coping is to try to be all things to all people. One person would say, I should smile more, another would say be happier, be sadder, be taller, be shorter. And I tried to play that game and I died. Booze worked for a while and then that quit working. So I went to rehab. This was a parish that put me on a pedestal and then tried to knock me down. The hope in all of that is that I went into rehab, and then I didn't run away so healing could happen in the parish as well as in me."

The tears were smarting in my eyes. But later I thought, Would he be less lonely if laypeople's ministry were more developed?

Mari said, at the end, "Once you become a priest, and I am sure you will, don't forget what it was like to be a layperson. So many priests forget."

In the second interview room, Jon Bruno greeted me again.

He was dressed in a white turtleneck and dark pants. It was a tiny room, barely large enough for Jon alone, much less for him, two other men, and me. A quiet priest who looked like a professor sat in one chair, his knees almost touching mine, and next to him was a young priest born in Singapore. Leng Lim had long thin fingers and a narrow face with high arched cheekbones. After a few pleasantries—How was the drive down? Did I need coffee?—Leng leaned forward and folded one beautiful hand into the other. "What are your thoughts, Nora," he said, "about creativity and priesthood? As a creative writer—and you are a writer—I mean, this is on my mind. When I was ordained, I decided to apply for jobs in the church that served the Asian communities, because I thought they would remind me of my family and friends back in Asia." Then he shook his head and made a small ironic grin. "And they have turned out to remind me of my aunts and uncles in more ways than one." He continued, "Don't get me wrong, the dysfunction is not Asians, nor Episcopalians. It's the entire church family. In my job, I find I have very little room to be creative, to be truly and fully *me*. Part of it is time; part of it is that there is very little mirroring that allows for Spirit to gush forth. I am always dealing with one crisis or another, or just the simple dysfunctions of fear and denial I remember from my own family."

Jon Bruno looked searchingly at Leng and then at me.

I said, "That is very much on my mind."

"I am worried about you," Leng said. "I know that some of my worry is projection on my part, but I know you are a creative person and the priesthood, as we now have it, does not offer much for such a one. I wish it did. Part of me wants you to become a priest in order to help that happen."

The room was still. None of us had anything more to say.

When the last interview was over, I drove home, mulling over what I had seen in those men and women who were priests.

Leng would leave his job shortly after our interview, and begin business school at Harvard. In two years, after Fred Borsch decided to retire, Jon Bruno would be consecrated bishop of the diocese of Los Angeles.

Shortly after I returned home, the phone rang. It was my "shepherd," a brilliant young priest who held a Ph.D. in theology and was soon to become the bishop's chaplain. He was calling on his new cell phone.

His voice was pitched with excitement. "I have the great pleasure of telling you," he said, "that the commission has voted unanimously . . ."

That night, I slept a deep wondrous sleep, waking now and then to bask in waves of relief. The next day, Sunday, after the ten o'clock service at Trinity, I was to read from my first book, a memoir about a year in faith at Trinity, which had just been published. At the coffee hour, George Barrett congratulated me on the commission's decision (he had written a reference), took me aside, and asked, in his hospitable growl, "Where do you plan to go to seminary?"

"I am not sure," I said. "I haven't had time to think about it."

"I think General [seminary in New York] would be good," he replied.

"Oh, I don't think so. I have actually walked around General and it seemed very old-boy to me."

"I think General would be excellent," he said, warming to his topic.

"It reminded me of St. John's," I said weakly. "And besides, they sent me a letter when I asked for their application that began, 'Dear Sir.' "

"General," George said meditatively. "Yes, I think General would be good for you."

"Right, George," I said. "I'll give it some thought."

Anne Howard took my hand and walked me into the guild

hall. "Today is the day that Nora's first book is published," she said, "and today is also the first day she woke up as a postulant for holy orders."

I stood at the podium. Mark Asman leaned against the wall at the far edge of the crowd. For twenty minutes, I read from that first book about a year in our lives together, a year when Kit was still alive, when Mark was new to Trinity, when Ann and I worked together in the soup kitchen then housed at Trinity. At the end, I read a section about the summer night the vestry voted to hire Mark as permanent rector of the parish. I read about how Steve Gibson had insisted on a vote that night, how Mark had protested, and then asked for a few minutes to himself. We had all walked around outside wondering what was going on with him. When we returned, he said to us, "I have been so used to being unacceptable all my life that I still can't believe I am accepted by you. I don't believe that you will still love me in the morning." I looked up at Mark and he put his hand to his face, and slipped out the door. I thought about his long discernment at Trinity, and our discernment as a congregation with him, and how the two are always intertwined.

He had said to me at our first meeting, "A priest must love herself."

I thought back on those weeks when Kit was dying. I thought about what Anne Strasburg gave me by coming up with the plan of travel. I thought of Vincent standing in my brother's yard surrounded by Kit's friends. Dickie Romero, driving my brother's body to the crematorium, and Donna, holding the basin of water at his memorial service.

What I know about love is that love is the power that makes things, that allows things to coalesce. Out of the pieces and shards of my brother's last hours, something was now knitted together. Beneath the chaos and horror of his death, there was a deep structure. It had coalesced.

It had coalesced because of what Anne Strasburg did for me,

and Dickie Romero, what Vincent and Rande and Donna and Kit's friends gave me. The discernment committees, the Commission on Ministry, Al Smith, and Mark Asman. They were, for me, the ongoing incarnation.

In the afternoon, I read at Chaucer's, our local independently owned bookstore. People packed into the aisles and sat on book tables. Mark stood outside in his clericals herding people in the door; Ann Jaqua brought me a glass of water; Perry Goodman, one of the children from Trinity, came up to me and said she thought the cover of the book was a very nice design. Just before I began to read, I remembered that this was the place I had had that profound encounter with the clerk and had realized that writing itself was a vocation. When I read out into the store, the quiet was like the quiet of a church. I thought, People make church; they carry with them the altar on which to place the sacrament of their lives.

By the end of the day, after a party for the book, I felt like a bride at too many of her own weddings and lucky to have so many choices.

I was free, now, to apply to seminary. But I had another book to write, for which I had signed a contract, this one.

Elizabeth's memorial service was held on the day I left for my book tour. "By nature and temperament, Elizabeth had clear ideas and a strong will," Basil Meeking said in his eulogy to her. "She would think things through, devise a strategy. Watching her plan a dinner party, select gifts, or just organizing me to go to the store, I could see in her skills what could have made her a statesman or a corporation president. Nothing escaped her. She knew what ought to be done, she told you in gentle, affectionate tones, and you did it."

I sat in the pew with all of the others who had known and loved her and knew that the cost of love is loss.

I traveled to a number of cities but it was in the Bay Area that something funny happened. I was to read at the Book Passage, in Larkspur, Marin County. The skies darkened early, the rain poured down. I was sure no one would show up. An old friend, Donald Schell, from St. John's College, who was now an Episcopal priest at St. Gregory's in San Francisco, had promised to drive up to Marin from the city; I had not seen him in twenty years.

I was deeply afraid of this reading without knowing why. Early in the evening, Vincent's father and stepmother met us for drinks next door to the bookstore. But I didn't sit with them. I spent that time sitting in a cubicle in the women's bathroom clutching my glow in the dark rosary, praying that I would not throw up, while women outside banged impatiently on the door. Finally, it was time and I crossed the courtyard, shielded from the rain by Vincent's cousin holding a London-made umbrella. There was a good crowd, and I read fine. But it was afterward when the turn came.

A woman in the back raised her hand. She asked me about a passage in that book in which we held a vigil at Trinity for the Jesuit priests who were killed in El Salvador. She was having trouble, I could make out, formulating her question.

"But was the whole community. . . . I am not sure how to ask this. . . ."

I waited. I said nothing. The room went quiet. We seemed to slow down all of us together, and then to cross a threshold while she worked at what she had to ask. I knew it was my job in that moment to hold us all in balance on the threshold so she could find her words.

"I am asking," she finally said, "was the whole community invited? I mean, everyone?"

"Yes," I said.

Afterward, after I signed a few books and we were standing around, a tall man walked over to Vincent and me. As he did, Vincent turned to me and said, "What happened there, when that woman asked about the community?"

"I can give it a guess," the man said, and I recognized Donald. We greeted each other and talked pleasantries and then he said, "Just to get back to what happened there. A priest is responsible not only for consecrating ordinary elements, but for consecrating ordinary life." He grinned and looked down at me.

"I don't think I've ever seen anyone preside at a book reading."

When the tour was over, Vincent and I came home and took a Saturday to go hiking along the Santa Ynez River in the county's backcountry. It was a beautiful day; the river was clear, and the winter grass was growing thick along the roadsides. On the way home, Vincent turned to me in the car.

"I want you to know that I think there is less of a gulf between us than I might have thought as to what we believe in," he said. "And I believe we can bridge whatever gulf there is."

On Sunday morning, I said to him, "I don't want to go to church."

He replied, "Call in secular."

We flew back to New Mexico for Christmas, to Las Cruces, in the south, where my parents had moved not long after Kit's death. Robert drove down from Polvadera to join all of us.

On the day before Christmas, I sat in the bar of the Hilton in Las Cruces watching ice hockey on the big-screen TV. A woman to my right said good-bye to her companion. She said, "Stay out of jail," and she wasn't joking. A few miles away, in Mesilla, men and women were shoveling sand into brown paper lunch sacks and placing votive candles in each one.

When the sacks were ready, they would set them on the roof and towers of Mesilla's church, on the sidewalks of the square, atop the adobe houses, and then light the votives inside. When I was growing up in Albuquerque, we set out luminarias each year. Kit and I climbed the ladder to the roof and my father directed us as to how far apart to place them. My mother told us that luminarias were lit to show the way for the Christ child to come.

And so I waited, as others were waiting. That night, we piled into the car and drove down to Mesilla to look at the luminarias. Lines of cars crept around the square, their lights dimmed or turned off. The light of hundreds of candles flickering through the soft ordinary brown of paper sacks made us all quiet. I imagined this: that whatever holiness there is at the heart of the world looked out on the luminarias, and placed its feet on the path they made, if only because the creatures who made them were so full of longing.

When I thought back on the last three years, it was as if I had crossed a series of invisible thresholds, passed through a series of new doors. When I visited the Bosque del Apache after Kit's death, I thought, He is alive. Now I think, So am I. This, as it turns out, is my resurrection story.

When I think about the resurrection now, I don't only think about what happened to Jesus. I think about what happened to his disciples. Something happened to them, too. They went into hiding after the crucifixion but after the resurrection appearances, they walked back out into the world. They became braver and stronger; they visited strangers, and healed the sick. As Nicholas Peter Harvey has pointed out in *Death's Gift*, it was not only what they saw when they saw Jesus, or how they saw it, but what was set free in them.

If there is some kind of life after death, what if it's not a life exclusively for the dead? What if it's a life available to us all, as Harvey argues, something the living can participate in, too? Just after someone has died, this life sometimes becomes briefly and intensely visible and what? Inhabitable? "The barrier between . . . two worlds grows very thin," said Stephen Vernay, a British writer who lost his wife to cancer. But then, Vernay added, "The appearances have to give way to something more important still, which is that we too can come alive . . . a new pattern of events is set free to happen around us."

We spend so much time in the church "believing" in the resurrection or "not believing" (six impossible things before breakfast) that we may lose the point. What if the resurrection is not about the appearances of Jesus alone but also about what those appearances pointed to, what they *asked*? And it is finally what we do with them that matters—make them into superstitions or use them as stepping stones to new life. We have to practice resurrection.

All of the work of discernment led me to this place. I had thought I was discerning a vocation to priesthood, but in fact I had been discerning my relation to my brother's death, to my husband, to the world I live in, and, finally, to myself. I had found the sacred, again, but in different places.

"It's like everything else, it has to start at the bottom," Ann Jaqua said. "It is like what happens in spiritual direction. You pay attention to things you never noticed. You start by thinking, There's something out there for me and I need to find it. In that search, there is nothing that isn't grist for the mill. And there will always be more of it, you are not going to outlive it. It's not going to run out."

I was not sure what I would do, finally. I was free to study for the priesthood. I had another book to write. Then it came to me, as I was writing these things down, in the act of writing, that I was meant to remain in the middle for a while, between clergy and laity, a hybrid, a crossbreed, not the one and not the other. An inhabitant of the borderlands, in order to inform not only myself but the church, too. I needed to live out the "priesthood of the laity" to find out how far it could be taken inside the church, and what it might mean outside her walls.

Understanding and developing the priesthood of the laity would have to lead to a redefinition of ordained priesthood, and a new relationship between the two that "acknowledges their interconnectedness," as William Countryman had said. The liturgical functions of both laity and clergy needed to be scrutinized, not because laypeople needed to be represented at the altar, as if they were filling a quota, but because what happens in liturgy should be symbolic of what happens in life. How had it been established that only priests serve the bread? What did serving the bread represent? By preaching in churches, I (and others) had broken a barrier that said only ordained persons could preach. At the Thursday-night Eucharist at Trinity, more and more laypersons were preaching. In the preaching of laypeople, we had heard a different set of stories than those told by priests, an intertwined double helix of faith and life in the world. What other liturgical functions could laypeople fill or share with ordained clergy? And how might this add to the life of the church?

Outside the church, the priesthood of the laity seemed to be about discerning when and how the work of laypersons was ministry, and what that ministry might need to develop, in order to "foreshadow the kingdom." How was my work as a writer a vocation? What did that vocation need, from the church, to flower in the world? What about other professions? How would we discern the vocational element or call in legal work, therapy, waitressing?

There was something about this that was like resurrection. It was an invitation; it asked.

I realized that even if I went very far as a layperson, I might find that, in the end, this inchoate longing that had hovered in and around me for these last years might very well turn out to be, yes, a call to ordained priesthood. There were many elements to it that matched what others saw as ordained priesthood, and many aspects of it that felt to me like ordained priesthood. But, because the priesthood of the laity was so neglected in the church, I knew now it was crucial to live it further out, so as to allow it to reveal itself, step by step.

"It wasn't a call," Ann Jaqua said. "It's a response."

It seemed to me, here in this borderland place, that the many priests I knew and respected, some of whom had interviewed me at the diocese, might welcome such an examination, such an incarnation, and so would many laypeople. And many would not.

"When it comes right down to it, it seems to me that Jesus invites us to follow where truth leads," my friend Margaret wrote in a recent sermon, "and to bear the cost of whatever truth we find."

What sustained me was the image of those early house churches and that company of friends. There is too great a gap between priest and layperson; I, at the moment, was living in that space. Here I was, awkward and ungainly, newly born.

Epilogue

I write this epilogue at the beginning of Lent, 2002.

Rande Brown is happy, and living in Polvadera. She counsels troubled teenagers.

Mark Asman is well and still at Trinity. The church thrives. Trinity has held two more same-gender marriages with no negative results.

Charles and Philip are happily married and have moved from Santa Barbara to a small town near Los Angeles.

Ann Jaqua is now on staff at Trinity as Coordinator for Shared Ministry, working on lay ministry development. She is about to form discernment committees to help laypersons decide their vocations in the world.

Al Smith has retired. He and his wife, Stephanie, live in San Diego, where Al is doing interim work in the church.

On November 25, 2000, George Barrett wrote a letter to the parish. He explained that four years before he'd had a failing of kidney function, and had decided to undergo dialysis. He explained that dialysis required time for treatment, a rigid diet, and heavy dependence on family and friends. And so, he wrote, "I have now come to the decision to end dialysis and face the inevitable death that will follow, be the time measured in days or weeks.

"I am at peace," he continued, "with trust in the God who does not manipulate events such as birth, sickness, success, failure, and death, but who is with us, suffering and rejoicing with us in all things and under all circumstances."

George died on December 3, 2000.

Three years have passed since I was made a postulant in the diocese of Los Angeles. I remain "in the gap" between priest and layperson. I continue to guest preach in churches in the West. In this time, several events stand out. In 1999, I flew to Indianapolis to take part in that city's Spirit and Place Conference. I read from my first book at Christ Church Cathedral, and afterward, in the question-and-answer session, someone asked me what I was doing these days, and I said I was considering a vocation to the priesthood. Later, a young woman lawyer drove me to the airport and said to me as we were touring a last bit of the city before leaving, "I want to say something to you that is probably out of line." I turned to look at her.

"I don't want you to be a priest," she said. "I don't mean you wouldn't be a good priest. But I am a layperson, trying to find my way in the church, and I need all the role models I can get."

In November 2001, I preached at Grace Church on Bainbridge Island, Washington, and the priest there, Bill Harper, said at the end of the service, "Nora, I want you to know. Your vocation is words."

Epilogue

That Christmas, I was asked by Anne Howard to serve the Eucharist bread on Christmas Eve. (The priest lined up to do the job had bowed out.)

I figured I would be safely tucked away at the back of the church for one of the largest services of the year, but at the rehearsal for the service, Mark Asman marched me over to where I was to stand: smack in front of the altar. I began to panic just then. I had worn what I hoped was modest, plain garb: a gray silk blouse and skirt with a black velvet coat over them. Just before the service began, I sat down in a pew near the altar, next to a woman in a wheelchair with a partially paralyzed face. She must have had a stroke. Even taking the stroke into account, she seemed somewhat cold and stiff. Her husband was very loving. The church was packed with people I didn't know. When it came time for communion, I got up and took the paten stacked with wafers from the acolyte and walked over to stand in front of the altar. I felt very much alone, without much to do. But gradually, the people starting coming forward, one by one. Serving the bread, as I have said before, is much slower than serving the wine. I had never served the bread at Trinity. I held the thin piece of wafer up to each person and said, "The Body of Christ. The Bread of Heaven." I looked in their eyes, unless they seemed to want not to look at anyone. They looked into my eyes. It was like a long gaze across a long gap, with the body of Christ in between. After a little while, a very short little while, I felt a small thrill of joy wash through me. I held the wafer up to a homeless man with no fingers on one hand, and said, "The Body of Christ. The Bread of Heaven," and then placed the wafer in his palm. His eyes were bright with tears. He stepped aside. The woman with the stroke rolled forward in her wheelchair, her husband pushing her. I looked in her eyes as I tucked the wafer into the hand bent in her lap and saw that all of her life was in her eyes and they were laughing. The people I was serving were all picking up on this feeling, whatever it was. Their eyes grinned. One of them almost giggled. The serving to each person became a little dance step, as if we were in a minuet, or one of those dances that involves a bow and a change of partners. A choir member, a child, a teenager with a tongue stud, a tattooed man, a woman with a haggard face and too much lipstick—the joy was all around us, running through us, and we were all a part of it, we were riding in it, we were dancing through it. I knew it was going on all the time and we were, that night, invited into it, we were adding to its strength. When I put down the empty paten, everything ended, just like that, and I walked back to my pew. It was good to walk back to the pew with the rest of the people, rather than take a place with the altar party. I thought to myself, I want to do that again. And then I thought, I wonder if God likes breaking the rules?

A few weeks ago, Mark Asman invited the small group of people at the Thursday Eucharist to join him at the altar, because, as he put it, "It is the people, it is all of us together who make the Eucharist." He showed us how to hold our hands in the orans position, the prayer position of arms bent at the elbow, palms in the air, and when to hold our palms over the bread and wine to bless them. It felt exactly right to do this, and for one of the few times in my life during communion I was not a spectator and my mind did not drift.

A friend of mine who is a priest talked with me about renouncing her orders, because she could no longer tolerate what she called the "clericalism" of the church, especially at the national level. Another priest, Michael Dwinell, in Portland, Maine, renounced his orders recently, having thought and prayed about it for some time. In a letter he wrote to friends, he said he found his ordination to be an "impediment" to his sense of his ongoing call.

"Vocation is about a relationship to the holy, first," Dwinell said in an interview, "and as that relationship deepens and expands a quality of intimacy and unpretentiousness is required; the role of official priest just gets in the way of that vulnerability.

"When you are a priest you have two masters, the church and God; the Episcopal Church perceives you as belonging to it. I am now more vocally theocentric than I was when I was ordained, more free to be that way because I no longer serve two masters and my connection feels uncluttered. It feels from the being, not from the role.

"Being a priest is being an agent of transformation," Dwinell continued. "Maybe the priest lifts up the sacrifice or is the sacrifice. It is knowing that every moment presents itself as a moment of transformation and midwifery is required, to be a participant witness and agent of that. To know moments are pregnant with that potentiality.

"An ordained priest at its best is someone who is willing to bear the visual imagery, to remind all of us of who we really are."

Vincent and I are in our second marriage to each other. We made more room for building up good times, at Vincent's suggestion, by taking every Wednesday off together after three in the afternoon. Yesterday, we hiked in the foothills and sat under some ponderosa pines near the edge of a canyon.

Two years ago, when the centuries changed, I officiated at a Taize service at Trinity, a simple service that does not require a priest, designed by the community of Taize, in France. It's a service of prayers and songs, most of which are in Latin, a language familiar to many Europeans. The songs are easy to sing and easy to memorize, being usually only one or two lines long.

It's a service that takes place mostly in candlelight, just the right way to celebrate the millennium.

Vincent and I went to a party together at a friend's house earlier in the evening. We took separate cars, and I left around 10:00 to go down to church and get ready for the service. It didn't feel very good leaving him on New Year's Eve. He said he might drop by before it started to wish me well.

The service began and I hadn't seen him.

We sang, "Veni sancte Spiritus": Come, Holy Spirit.

At the intercessions, people called out prayers into the dark:

> For my brother, leaving for Germany;
> For my father, known as Bop;
> For Barbara, whose dog has died;
> For E., who needs a liver transplant

A litany, a chain of lives.

A woman sat in a pew with a child stretched out sleeping beside her.

At the peace, at the stroke of midnight, Stefani Schatz, who was a seminarian at the time and is now ordained, and I went down the aisle, and wished everyone peace and happy new year. I was nearly at the end of my side of the aisle when I looked up and there was Vincent, smiling, open, and intimate. "Happy New Year," he said, and we kissed.

When I came home later that night, he said he had come to the church to say hello to me, later than he thought, and Iva Schatz, Stefani's mother, was standing at the door and she handed him a bulletin and he was too afraid of Iva to turn around and leave. He said that he had liked the service of Taize very much. He had never been to one before. He liked the singing and the silence, he said; it was a combination of "Catholic and Quaker." He especially liked the songs in Latin. "It's funny," he said. "I can't sing 'Lord, we adore you,' but I can sing, 'Adoramus te domine.' " And he liked it, he said gently, because there were no priests.

As we sat in the bedroom talking, I thought, If anything, "my vocation" is to find ways for the church to speak to people like Vincent, the one person in the world to whom I want always to speak.

ACKNOWLEDGMENTS

With thanksgiving for the life of David Gallagher.

My thanks to my editor, Jane Garrett, and my agent, Flip Brophy.

Thanks to Harriet Barlow and Ben Strader; Elise Kyllo, Randy Roberson, and everyone at the Blue Mountain Center; Peter Barnes and Mark Dowie at the Mesa Refuge; and the MacDowell Colony.

To my brothers: Timothy Jolley, Robert Hagler, Nick Radelmiller, Andrew Colquhoun, Laurence Harms, Allan Smith, William Brown, Roy Parker, and Robert Sevensky.

Mark Asman, Ann Jaqua, Anne Howard, Mari Mitchel, Anthony Guillén, Mark Kowalewski, Jon Bruno, Mark Grotke, Kay Sylvester, Mark Gardner, Charles Cook, and Michael Dwinell.

Ellin Barret, Jamie Barret-Riley, Margaret Bullitt-Jonas, Dane Goodman, Cynthia Gorney, Jodie Ireland, Andra Lichtenstein, Anne Makepeace, Ellen Meloy, David Morris, Patrick Riley, Marie Schoeff, and Anne Strasburg.

A special thanks to Asa Calthorpe.

Thanks to and for my cousins, Nan and Craig Merrill, and Sally McKenzie.

Thank you to Julie, Robert, and Sean Gallagher.

And, always, thanks to and for Vincent Stanley.

ALSO BY NORA GALLAGHER

THINGS SEEN AND UNSEEN

A Year Lived in Faith

It started with an occasional Sunday, a "tourist's" visit to a local church. Eventually Nora Gallagher entered into a yearlong journey to discover her faith and a relationship with God. Whether writing about her brother's battle against cancer, talking to homeless men about the World Series, serving communion wine, or questioning the afterlife, Gallagher draws us into a world of journeys and mysteries that are grounded in a gritty reality. Using the Christian calendar as her compass, she braids together the events of a year in one church and her own spiritual journey. Gallagher calls into focus "the world of the almost unknown" as she writes of faith and its meaning, uncertainty and suffering, grace and commitment in this harrowingly honest memoir. Thought provoking and profoundly perceptive, *Things Seen and Unseen* is a remarkable demonstration that "the road to the sacred is paved with the ordinary."

"The deep serenity that suffuses Gallagher's work, the lyrical cadences in which she writes, do not blunt the sharp edges of what she discovers in her quest for meaning."
—*Los Angeles Times*

Religion/Spirituality/0-679-77549-8

VINTAGE BOOKS
Available at your local bookstore, or call toll-free to order:
1-800-793-2665 (credit cards only).